The Confucian Concept of Learning

What does the Confucian heritage mean to modern East Asian education today? Is it invalid and outdated, or an irreplaceable cultural resource for an alternative approach to education? And to what extent can we recover the humanistic elements of the Confucian tradition of education for use in world education?

Written from a comparative perspective, this book attempts to collectively explore these pivotal questions in search of future directions in education. In East Asian countries like China, Japan, Korea and Taiwan, Confucianism as a philosophy of learning is still deeply embedded in the ways people think of and practice education in their everyday life, even if their official language puts on the Western scientific mode. It discusses how Confucian concepts including rite, rote-learning and conformity to authority can be differently understood for the post-liberal and post-metaphysical culture of education today. The contributors seek to make sense of East Asian experiences of modern education, and to find a way to make Confucian philosophy of education compatible with the Western idea of liberal education.

This book was originally published as a special issue of *Educational Philosophy and Theory*.

Duck-Joo Kwak is Professor of Philosophy of Education at Seoul National University, Korea. She is the author of *Education for Self-transformation: Essay as an Educational Practice* (2011) and numerous articles on values education and teacher education.

Morimichi Kato is Professor of Philosophy of the Faculty of Human Sciences at Sophia University, Japan. He has a long-standing interest in the history of Platonism and humanism in the West, and has written extensively on Plato, Aristotle, Cicero, Renaissance philosophers, Heidegger, Charles Taylor and Gianni Vattimo.

Ruyu Hung is Professor of Philosophy of Education at National Chiayi University, Taiwan. She is the author of *Leaning Nature* (2010), *Education between Speech and Writing: Crossing the Boundaries of Dao and Deconstruction* (2017) and many other philosophical and educational articles.

Educational Philosophy and Theory
Series Editor: Peter Roberts, University of Canterbury, New Zealand

This series is devoted to cutting-edge scholarship in educational philosophy and theory. Each book in the series focuses on a key theme or thinker and includes essays from a range of contributors. To be published in the series, a book will normally have first appeared as a special issue of *Educational Philosophy and Theory*, one of the premier philosophy of education journals in the world. This provides an assurance for readers of the quality of the work and enhances the visibility of the book in the international philosophy of education community. Books in this series combine creativity with rigour and insight. The series is intended to demonstrate the value of diverse theoretical perspectives in educational discourse, and contributors are invited to draw on literature, art and film as well as traditional philosophical sources in their work. Questions of educational policy and practice will also be addressed. The books published in this series will provide key reference points for subsequent theoretical work by other scholars, and will play a significant role in advancing philosophy of education as a field of study.

Titles in the series include:

Philosophy in Schools
Edited by Felicity Haynes

New Directions in Educational Leadership Theory
Edited by Scott Eacott and Colin W. Evers

Expertise, Pedagogy and Practice
Edited by David Simpson and David Beckett

Philosophy and Pedagogy of Early Childhood
Edited by Sandy Farquhar and E. Jayne White

The Dilemma of Western Philosophy
Edited by Michael A. Peters and Carl Mika

Educational Philosophy and New French Thought
Edited by David R. Cole and Joff P.N. Bradley

Activating Aesthetics
Edited by Elizabeth M. Grierson

Levinas and the Philosophy of Education
Edited by Guoping Zhao

The Confucian Concept of Learning
Revisited for East Asian Humanistic Pedagogies
Edited by Duck-Joo Kwak, Morimichi Kato and Ruyu Hung

A Kaleidoscopic View of Chinese Philosophy of Education
Edited by Ruyu Hung

John Dewey's Democracy and Education in an Era of Globalization
Edited by Mordechai Gordon and Andrea R. English

The Confucian Concept of Learning

Revisited for East Asian Humanistic Pedagogies

Edited by
Duck-Joo Kwak, Morimichi Kato and Ruyu Hung

LONDON AND NEW YORK

First published 2018
by Routledge
2 Park Square, Milton Park, Abingdon, Oxon, OX14 4RN, UK

and by Routledge
711 Third Avenue, New York, NY 10017, USA

Routledge is an imprint of the Taylor & Francis Group, an informa business

© 2018 Philosophy of Education Society of Australasia

All rights reserved. No part of this book may be reprinted or reproduced or utilised in any form or by any electronic, mechanical, or other means, now known or hereafter invented, including photocopying and recording, or in any information storage or retrieval system, without permission in writing from the publishers.

Trademark notice: Product or corporate names may be trademarks or registered trademarks, and are used only for identification and explanation without intent to infringe.

British Library Cataloguing in Publication Data
A catalogue record for this book is available from the British Library

ISBN13: 978-1-138-48919-6

Typeset in Plantin
by RefineCatch Limited, Bungay, Suffolk

Publisher's Note
The publisher accepts responsibility for any inconsistencies that may have arisen during the conversion of this book from journal articles to book chapters, namely the possible inclusion of journal terminology.

Disclaimer
Every effort has been made to contact copyright holders for their permission to reprint material in this book. The publishers would be grateful to hear from any copyright holder who is not here acknowledged and will undertake to rectify any errors or omissions in future editions of this book.

Contents

Citation Information — vii
Notes on Contributors — ix

Introduction: The Confucian Concept of Learning Revisited for East Asian Humanistic Pedagogies — 1
Duck-Joo Kwak, Morimichi Kato and Ruyu Hung

1. Ethics of Learning and Self-knowledge: Two cases in the Socratic and Confucian teachings — 7
Duck-Joo Kwak

2. Humanistic Traditions, East and West: Convergence and divergence — 23
Morimichi Kato

3. "The Source of Learning is Thought" Reading the *Chin-ssu lu* with a "Western Eye" — 36
Roland Reichenbach

4. A Theory of Learning in Confucian Perspective — 52
Chung-ying Cheng

5. The Corporeality of Learning: Confucian Education in Early Modern Japan — 64
Masashi Tsujimoto

6. *Lixue*, the Lost Art: Confucianism as a form of cultivation of mind — 75
Hyong-Jo Han

7. A Critique of Confucian Learning: On Learners and Knowledge — 85
Ruyu Hung

8. Two Concerns of the Confucian Learner — 97
Youn-Ho Park

9. Modern Versus Tradition: Are there two different approaches to reading of the Confucian classics? — 106
Chung-yi Cheng

Index — 119

Citation Information

The chapters in this book were originally published in *Educational Philosophy and Theory*, volume 48, issue 1 (January 2016). When citing this material, please use the original page numbering for each article, as follows:

Introduction
The Confucian Concept of Learning Revisited for East Asian Humanistic Pedagogies
Duck-Joo Kwak, Morimichi Kato and Ruyu Hung
Educational Philosophy and Theory, volume 48, issue 1 (January 2016) pp. 1–6

Chapter 1
Ethics of Learning and Self-knowledge: Two cases in the Socratic and Confucian teachings
Duck-Joo Kwak
Educational Philosophy and Theory, volume 48, issue 1 (January 2016) pp. 7–22

Chapter 2
Humanistic Traditions, East and West: Convergence and divergence
Morimichi Kato
Educational Philosophy and Theory, volume 48, issue 1 (January 2016) pp. 23–35

Chapter 3
"The Source of Learning is Thought" Reading the Chin-ssu lu with a "Western Eye"
Roland Reichenbach
Educational Philosophy and Theory, volume 48, issue 1 (January 2016) pp. 36–51

Chapter 4
A Theory of Learning in Confucian Perspective
Chung-ying Cheng
Educational Philosophy and Theory, volume 48, issue 1 (January 2016) pp. 52–63

Chapter 5
The Corporeality of Learning: Confucian Education in Early Modern Japan
Masashi Tsujimoto
Educational Philosophy and Theory, volume 48, issue 1 (January 2016) pp. 64–74

CITATION INFORMATION

Chapter 6
Lixue (Ihak) the Lost Art: Confucianism as a form of cultivation of mind
Hyong-Jo Han
Educational Philosophy and Theory, volume 48, issue 1 (January 2016) pp. 75–84

Chapter 7
A Critique of Confucian Learning: On Learners and Knowledge
Ruyu Hung
Educational Philosophy and Theory, volume 48, issue 1 (January 2016) pp. 85–96

Chapter 8
Two Concerns of the Confucian Learner
Youn-Ho Park
Educational Philosophy and Theory, volume 48, issue 1 (January 2016) pp. 97–105

Chapter 9
Modern Versus Tradition: Are there two different approaches to reading of the Confucian classics?
Chung-yi Cheng
Educational Philosophy and Theory, volume 48, issue 1 (January 2016) pp. 106–118

For any permission-related enquiries please visit:
http://www.tandfonline.com/page/help/permissions

Notes on Contributors

Chung-ying Cheng is Professor of Philosophy at the University of Hawaii at Manoa, USA. His research areas are Chinese Philosophy (Confucianism and Neo-Confucianism, Yijing) and contemporary Western Philosophy (philosophy of language, philosophical hermeneutics, Peirce, Quine and Kant). He is the founder and chief editor of the *Journal of Chinese Philosophy*.

Hyong-Jo Han is Professor of Philosophy at the Academy of Korean Studies in Seoul, Korea, where he teaches Korean Confucianism, Chinese Classics and Zen Buddhism. His books include *Buddha's Fatal Joke: An Invitation to Diamond Sutra* (2011) and *Why Joseon Confucianism Today?* (2008). His writing and speaking focuses on the contemporary meaning of Confucianism for the general public.

Ruyu Hung is Professor of Philosophy of Education at National Chiayi University, Taiwan. She is the author of *Leaning Nature* (2010), *Education between Speech and Writing: Crossing the Boundaries of Dao and Deconstruction* (2017) and many other philosophical and educational articles.

Morimichi Kato is Professor of Philosophy of the Faculty of Human Sciences at Sophia University, Japan. He has a long-standing interest in the history of Platonism and humanism in the West, and has written extensively on Plato, Aristotle, Cicero, Renaissance philosophers, Heidegger, Charles Taylor and Gianni Vattimo.

Duck-Joo Kwak is Professor of Philosophy of Education at Seoul National University, Korea. She is the author of *Education for Self-transformation: Essay as an Educational Practice* (2011) and numerous articles on values education and teacher education.

Youn-Ho Park is Professor of the Department of Education at the Gwangju National University of Education, Republic of Korea. His research interests are in the fields of history of Korean education, Confucianism and libertarianism. He is a past president of the Korean Society for History of Education.

Roland Reichenbach is Professor of Education at the University of Zürich, Switzerland. He is the president of the Swiss Society of Educational Research, vice president of the (International) Society of Education and Knowledge, and editor of the *Zeitschrift für Pädagogik*. His main interests are educational theory, pedagogical ethics, citizenship education, negotiation and education.

Masashi Tsujimoto is a Professor at National Taiwan University. He has published *Kinsei kyōiku shisūshi no kenkyō [Research on the history of early modern educational thought]* (1990) and *Shisō to kyōiku no mediashi [History of Intellectual and Educational Media]* (2011).

The Confucian Concept of Learning Revisited for East Asian Humanistic Pedagogies

Duck-Joo Kwak, Morimichi Kato & Ruyu Hung

This special issue on the Confucian concept of learning was self-consciously, if not self-critically, framed by scholars in the field of philosophy of education whose cultural roots lie in the East Asian tradition of Confucianism. The materials are the outcome of a workshop funded by Harvard Yenching Institute, a research institute well known for its studies of Asian culture. This workshop is said to be organized at a culturally dynamic and turbulent moment on the world stage in which, Asia, *as* a region is emerging as a new economic power affected by China's rapid growth. This development tends to draw people's attention at this time to the scholarship on educational thoughts and practice of the eastern tradition. The tendency may be more directly motivated by high academic performance of K-12 students from East Asian countries in international comparative tests. Or more profoundly, it may be motivated by the pursuit of an alternative model to the troubled practice of the scientific model for teaching and learning in modern schooling. Or more broadly, it may just be a public response to global demands for cross-cultural understanding in rapidly shifting economic and political environments.

Though the study of Confucianism has a long-established tradition in East Asia, much of it is historical and philological in nature. In the field of Educational Sciences, which is still dominated by the modern Enlightenment perspective, Confucianism is usually considered as outdated even in this region. But the Confucian concept of learning has played an important role in everyday school culture of the East Asian countries since Confucius placed learning (學) at the very center of his teaching. Even after the introduction of Western education into these countries, the traditional Confucian features of learning retained some of its influence on the educational practice of East Asian countries. Among others, what follows are those that are still of great relevance to today's school practice in East Asian countries:

- The practice of the Rite (*li*, 禮) that is often confounded with 'formalities' but is a sort of body-knowledge.
- The method of memorization that is often seen as 'rote learning' but can have a deeper significance as a method of learning.
- The conformity to norms and authority as a method of self-discipline.

- The broader understanding of the self that goes beyond the individual self of the modern West.

These can be said to constitute important yet contestable resources for the contemporary education of humanistic/liberal learning shared by the countries in the East Asian region.

Given this cultural background, it is notable that there have seldom been substantial academic exchanges among educational scholars in this region for a collective effort to tackle their shared educational problems and difficulties, which they often confront in the process of educational modernization in the last century of their modern history. Thus, whatever the reason for this may have been, it appears quite urgent for scholars in East Asian countries to meet and discuss some features of Confucian learning and its tradition in relation to modern schooling and education for their possible contribution to, or danger for, contemporary education in the late-modern culture. In what follows, we will specify our initial objectives for the workshop and discuss how the objectives were met, although not without some challenges. This will allow readers to have a better sense of the general concerns of the authors of this special issue as well as a narrower focus on dealing with the Confucian concept of learning. We will also add some questions and issues which occurred more than once during the workshop, from which we can derive some direction for our future research in regard to the Confucian idea of learning and education.

First, we aimed to pursue the encounter between scholarship in East Asian philosophy and scholarship in philosophy of education, in order to find some ways of reformulating the Confucian idea of learning in such a way as to conceptualize and make sense of people's *educational experiences* in East Asian countries. This aim presupposes that a similar pattern of school experiences may be shared by most East Asians due to their shared tradition of Confucianism and history of westernization. This pattern has to do with two competing educational values common in their school culture, namely historically rooted traditional Confucian values, on one hand, and recently imported western liberal values, on the other hand. The trouble with this school culture is that the two values are mixed in such an *estranged* manner that it often leaves the minds of East Asian students split between the two different logics and moralities of competing cultures. Thus, our attempt to *make sense* of these confusing and ambiguous school experiences in the minds of East Asians requires us to take a look at their learning experiences through the lens of the background worldview that they bring with them. We think this sort of interpretive inquiry on the Confucian idea of learning from the perspective of the insiders can contribute to developing a modernized Confucian model of humanist pedagogy, a model which would be indigenous to the regional culture; it would also contribute to the enrichment of language for the discourse on humanistic/liberal education, which falls into peril due to the dominance of the dehumanizing scientific model in teaching and learning.

Second, we explored a feasible framework through which we could compare the two seemingly contrasting philosophies of liberal learning of the Eastern and Western tradition of the humanities: formality vs. free-thinking, conformity vs. independence, or obedience vs. autonomy. It requires that we seek the question of what makes 'liberal learning' genuinely *liberal*, which is likely to lead into a broader concept of an *educational* perspective shared by the two traditions. Through the workshop, we were able to formulate this educational perspective with the term 'ethics of (liberal) learning'; for the Confucian idea of learning allows us to view '(liberal) learning' *as* a meta-virtue which motivates us to *become virtuous* and thereby to shape our ethical selfhood. Thus, the idea of '*ethics* of (liberal) learning' or the idea of 'learning as a *meta-virtue*' can be further developed as a possible hermeneutical framework through which the two humanistic traditions of East and West are to be meaningfully compared.

Third, the workshop provided scholars from different East Asian countries with an opportunity to exchange their ideas and interpretations on their own Confucian tradition of learning for mutual understanding. This attempt was something radically new, given that most East Asian philosophers of education had had a strong tendency to look at the West for their model, while possessing lamentably poor knowledge of the East Asian heritage common to them. This workshop enabled them to realize that one of the common heritages for them was their deep-rooted respect for learning as a human virtue. Thus, we notice that such topics as 'the rite' (禮) in its relation to one's bodily orientation, the importance of 'thinking' or 'reflection' (思) in one's learning, the concept of Junzi (君子) as the educated man and the concept of ren (仁) as the highest principle of Confucian ethics of learning, appear time and again throughout most of the authors' works presented at the workshop. However, the workshop also revealed acute differences among different East Asian countries in their emphases on aspects of the Confucian tradition of learning. For example, the scholarly or intellectualistic tradition of Neo-Confucianism has been more dominant in Korean culture, whereas more of the literary tradition of Confucianism as a critique of the intellectualistic Neo-Confucianism seems to have been preferred in Japanese culture. Comparative studies across different East Asian countries for the differences in their Confucian traditions seem to be necessary not only for mutual understanding but also for cultural self-understanding.

The workshop has also raised some unexpected yet much sharper and intriguing questions for our future study on the Confucian tradition of education. For example, the question of how to read Confucian classical texts came to the surface: a *philosophical* reading vs. an *existential* reading. It also made us aware of two distinctive modes of learning from the Confucian tradition: learning *as an art of living* (古學) and learning *as cultivation of the heart-mind* (心學), which are in tension. Furthermore, as to the purpose of learning in the Confucian tradition, we noticed that there has always been a tension between 'learning-for-oneself' and 'learning-for-others'. The tensions may be of a kind that is supposed to be kept or lived, rather than to be overcome, by the actual lives of Confucian learners. Yet, how to be able to do so may deserve serious attention and scholarly talk as an educational matter.

This special issue includes nine essays, divided into three different categories of sub-questions. The first two essays address the question, 'Why is the Confucian concept of learning to be revisited?' Here, readers may be exposed to comparative perspectives on the concept of learning, Eastern and Western. Undertaking a philosophical analysis in her essay 'Ethics of Learning and Self-knowledge: two cases in the Socratic and Confucian teachings', Duck-Joo Kwak makes a comparison between Socratic and Confucian concepts of learning in terms of the idea of self-knowledge that both thinkers strongly highlight in their philosophy. Here, she makes an issue of the commonly accepted contrast between Socrates and Confucian in the way they do philosophy. For Socrates, a philosopher as a wisdom-seeker is the one who is always *critical* and *skeptical* to what is given to him or her, whereas, for Confucian, Junzi (君子) as an ideal learner is the one who knows how to *conform to* the given norms and values. While acknowledging this difference between them in general, Kwak attempts to show how the contrast may not be as sharp as it first appears and to explore the common moral concerns underlying their differences. Secondly, Morimich Kato sketches out the two traditions of the humanities, Eastern and Western, with an intellectual historical perspective in his essay 'Humanistic Traditions, East and West: Convergence and Divergence'. He compares the eastern and western traditions of humanities in its similarities and dissimilarities. He especially focuses on the literary tradition of Japanese Confucianism on one hand, and the Roman and Renaissance Humanism's emphasis on the rhetoric and language studies on the other hand. This essay will be intriguing, especially to readers who are unfamiliar with the eastern tradition of Confucian humanism, helping them better understand their own culture in comparison to the East.

The second part of this issue addresses the question, 'How can we reconstruct the educational ideas in the Confucian philosophy of learning?' Roland Reichenbach's essay, 'the Source of Learning is Thought: Reading the Chin-ssu lu (近思錄) with a Western eye', is calmly seductive as an exploratory paper on Neo-Confucian thought from a western perspective. His essay is poetic in the sense that readers, while reading through it, tend to contemplate on Zhu Xi's (朱熹) words in relation to their lives. Another strength is his association of the Neo-Confucian idea of learning as self-transformative with the German notion of *Bildung*, which has always fascinated the Confucian-minded philosophers of education in the East Asian region. The author exemplifies a way of conversing with two cultures in his own voice, albeit in an exploratory form. We think this essay can be a good introduction for western readers who are completely new to Neo-Confucian thoughts and ideas. The second paper by Chung-Ying Cheng entitled 'A Theory of Learning in Confucian Perspective' is a more comprehensive and theoretical account of the Confucian concept of learning. This piece would well serve those who are already familiar with Confucian texts and ideas, since it lays out a conceptual picture of the Confucian idea of learning in a more systematic manner. On the other hand, Masashi Tsujimoto's essay, 'the Corporeality of Learning: Confucian Education in early Modern Japan', is an educationally fascinating and well-informed historical paper that details the corporeal aspect of the Confucian practice of learning. As we said earlier, even if there are some commonalities in their Confucian traditions across the different Confucian countries of East Asia, each country historically adopted the tradition from China in a different way. Tsujimoto's paper effectively reveals the differences in the Japanese version, which attaches a high spiritual value to the formality in their bodily movement pervasive in its culture. This discussion of the corporeal aspect of Confucian learning can be interestingly contrasted with Foucault's account of the disciplinary nature of knowledge acquisition in the modern period of the West. Lastly, Hyong-Jo Han's essay, entitled 'Lixue, the Lost Art: Confucianism as a Form of Cultivation of Mind', is an insightful and poetic introduction to a version of Korean Confucianism. This essay succeeds in giving readers a sense of what Korean Confucianism is like for the Koreans, especially its contemplative and inward-looking character as a way of cultivating their heart-minds. While informing readers of a version of Korean Confucianism, it blesses the readers with moments of reflection on life and education.

The last section addresses the question: 'What can the Confucian heritage of educational ideas mean to the late-modern contemporary world: critique, tension and reconnection?' Ruyu Hung's paper entitled, 'A Critique of the Confucian Learning: On Learners and Knowledge' is a critical review of the Confucian tradition of learning, especially its hierarchical classification of four different capacities of learners and its exclusive concern with *ethical* knowledge. The criticism sounds a bit ahistorical, but contains in it something worth listening to especially for those who want to see how the Confucian tradition of learning can be made relevant and adapted to the contemporary culture of education in the East and West. On the other hand, Youn-ho Park in his essay 'Two Concerns of the Confucian Learner' brings out two key concepts, which has been long neglected, yet embedded in the Confucian tradition of education, namely, 'learning-for-oneself' and 'learning-for-others'. Then, he makes use of them to diagnose one cause of contemporary educational malaise in modern Korea, that is, exam-obsessed knowledge education. In other words, he attempts to find a way to understand an educational phenomenon in modern Korea by tracing it back to its long Confucian tradition and culture. The attempt is original and his underlying view is powerful in that he tries to look into the Confucian tradition to find a framework through which we can understand our current educational problem, while assuming a more ambivalent attitude toward the tradition itself. Lastly, Chung-Yi Cheng's essay, 'Modern versus Traditional: Are there two different approaches to reading of the Confucian Classics', raises an educationally important and challenging question in regard to how to teach and read classical Confucian texts in such a way as to make them *alive* and *relevant* to our contemporary young readers. His argument in defense of 'philosophical' and 'existential' approaches is solid and plausible, even if needing to be further developed in order for it to be employed for our actual practice of teaching and reading. In our view, his account of existential reading is educationally more attractive and deserves more attention since it emphasizes *active* and *personal* reading, which is perceived as lacking with rule conforming East Asian students. This also imposes a practical or ethical force upon those who are engaged in reading, and in that sense it well represents the ethics of (humanistic) reading.

We hope this series of papers will smoothly and gradually guide readers, who are unfamiliar with Confucian texts, into the world of a different educational tradition and moral universe. But to make that journey even easier, in what follows, we will prepare potential readers with brief information on the Confucian texts, scholars, and concepts that the readers may frequently encounter in reading the papers in this issue. We want to conclude this introduction with a special thanks to the editorial board of the journal, who allowed this special issue to come to fruition. Their concern and appreciation for cultural differences and intercultural understanding is itself to be highly regarded and appreciated, since we are living in the world where such intellectual and moral virtues tend to be so easily put aside in favor of more practical and exchangeable utilities even in the field of education.

Classical Texts of Confucianism: The Four Books

the Analects (論語)
the Mencius (猛者)
the Great Learning (大学)
the Doctrine of the Mean (中庸)

Zhu Xi and His Books

Zhu Xi (朱熹 1130–1120): one of the most influential rationalist Neo-Confucian scholars from the Song dynasty of China, who established a tradition which assigned a special significance to the above four books as the classical texts of Confucianism.
the Chin-ssu lu (*Reflections on Things at Hand*, 近思錄)
The Complete Works of Master Zhu (朱子大全)
Classified Conversations of Master Zhu (朱子語類)

Important Confucian Terms

xue (學, learning)
junzi (君子, a learned man, a self-ruling man)
shengxian (圣贤, sagely person)
ren (仁, humanity, benevolence, goodness as the highest principle of Confucian virtues)
li (禮, rites, ritual propriety)
dao (道, the Way)
tian (天, Heaven)
wen (文, cultured forms of human expression and language)

Duck-Joo Kwak
Morimichi Kato
Ruyu Hung

Ethics of Learning and Self-knowledge: Two cases in the Socratic and Confucian teachings

DUCK-JOO KWAK

Abstract

This paper attempts to do a comparative study on two traditions of humanistic pedagogies, West and East, represented by the Socratic and the Confucian teachings. It is intended to put into question our common misunderstanding reflected in the stereotyped contrasts between the Socratic self and the Confucian self: an intellectualist vs. a moralist, an active vs. a passive learner, and a political progressive vs. a political conservative. In this attempt, I will focus on the clarification of the idea of 'self-knowledge' in each thinker, especially in its connection to our being virtuous or good. This bold attempt will give us a chance to view Socratic and Confucian teachings from an unfamiliar perspective, which will in turn lead us to see where and how the two thinkers' teachings can converge and diverge in a new light for our humanistic teaching. It will also show how a comparative study in philosophy of education can contribute to constructive intercultural conversations.

1. Introduction: Two Different Ethics of Learning from Two Traditions

The Anglo-European discourse around 'the end of philosophy' in the late twentieth century has brought up a big shift in the notion of philosophy from a *theoretical* pursuit for truth into praxis, i.e. an activity for *practical* wisdom or even an art of living, as more clearly specified by Richard Rory and Michel Foucault among others. This shift resonates of the ancient notion of philosophy well capsulated in Blumenbeg's expression, 'since ancient times theory (philosophy) was supposed to make life happy' (Blumenberg, 1983, p. 232). It also seems to be aligned to the Confucian notion of 'learning' (學) as a whole-hearted pursuit of tao (道), the way to become 'a good person' represented by a noble man (君子) or a sage (聖人). I suspect that what always drew my East Asian sensibility into the tradition of western philosophy might be the semblance between these two ancient notions of philosophy in their fundamental spirit, namely their common orientation in which 'ethics' (or philosophy as ethics) is essentially associated to 'learning'. This means that learning for both traditions is considered inherently associated with a matter of how to find the right way to conduct our lives to become good persons. The best thinkers who represent this orientation from the two traditions can be said to be Socrates and Confucius.

However, the commonality of both traditions appears to end here in most of comparative studies on two traditions, East and West. For example, Li (2012) makes a sharp contrast between two traditions on the concept of learning in her book *Cultural Foundations of Learning*. Rightly pointing out that the idea of learning has *cultural* foundations, she claims that in following the Socratic tradition, the West values the rational individual mind that is trained to interrogate the world and become its master, whereas, based on the Confucian tradition, the East values learning for a moral virtue and moral self-perfection. In other words, Westerners tend to define learning *cognitively*, while Asians tend to define it *morally*. Here Jin Li seems to underestimate the ethical nature and implication of the Socratic teaching by being too much focused on the cultural differences supposedly derived from the Socratic and Confucian traditions.

Yu (2005) is more subtle on this issue in her paper entitled 'the beginning of ethics: Confucius and Socrates'. She claims that both thinkers are the founders of ethics for each tradition and attempt to link doing ethics with learning virtues. But, according to Yu, they differ about what the virtues are and how to pursue them. A distinct difference between them, Yu notes, that they had different attitudes toward their given traditional and social values. Socrates appears to be critical of them in encouraging his interlocutors to call them into question, and Confucius cherishes them as a cultural transmitter, instructing his disciples to conform to them. In Yu's conclusion (2005, pp. 184–185), for Socrates, ethics and learning are a matter of critical examination of one's moral beliefs in pursuit of virtue as an intellectual process; and for Confucius, they are a matter of acquiring and practicing a unified right moral knowledge in pursuit of virtue as a full-fledged development of moral character. This tells us that, for both thinkers, the purpose of learning lies in acquiring moral virtues, but that the moral virtues are differently defined, especially in their relations to given traditional and social values.

However, I wonder how legitimate or even useful this sort of contrasting approaches, which are framed to seek *dichotomies* between the two cultures, may be. It is likely to lead us either into an unsound yet convenient attribution of their relevance to modern pedagogies or an easy acceptance of cultural relativism. Thus, following Michael Peters' suggestion on how to do comparative studies, I try to 'begin with a robust comparison of the question of self-knowledge construed as questions of "knowing oneself" in Socrates and (as questions of) "its relation to the Other" in Confucius' (Peters, 2015). This is an approach with the assumption that both thinkers address the same question, namely 'How should we live?', and end up with an analogous answer, that is 'self-knowledge'. This is to say that both ethics of learning in Socratic and Confucian teachings aspire for the acquisition of self-knowledge, which is a form of moral knowledge that affects us as moral beings.

This paper will consist of two parts: the Socratic teaching and the Confucian teaching. This attempt is motivated to put into question our common misunderstanding reflected in the stereotyped contrasts between the Socratic self and the Confucian self: an intellectualist vs. a moralist, an active vs. a passive learner, a political progressive vs. a political conservative, and so on. In this attempt, I will focus on the clarification of the idea of 'self-knowledge' in each thinker, especially in its connection to our being virtuous or good. I think that this bold attempt will give us a chance to see Socratic and Confucian teachings from a new and unfamiliar perspective, which will in turn lead us to see where and how the two thinkers' teachings can converge and diverge in a new light.

2. Socratic Teaching for Self-knowledge: Critical Thinking as a Way to *Understand* Moral Knowledge

We often compare two seemingly contrasting features of liberal learning between the Eastern and Western traditions: formality vs. free-thinking, conformity vs. independence, or obedience vs. autonomy. To what extent may this contrasting view be valid? 'Critical and independent thinking' has been considered one of key educational aims for good citizenship in the West. The public school in the West aims to lead young students to struggle against the uncritical acceptance of their moral habits and opinions that have shaped their character from early on in their childhood. Critical thinking is regarded as both an ability and disposition to question their given moral knowledge on what is right to believe or to do, which they have relied upon to find their way around the social world. The questioning usually goes: *On what ground* do you believe this to be right?; *What do you mean* by what you say? It asks students to *spell out* the (logical or empirical) grounds or meanings of their moral beliefs *into words*. This is the demand to *revisit* what we already know and to make a distance from it. Socrates is considered the first *liberal* thinker in the West who invented this critical thinking (Nussbaum, 1997, 2010).

What is the educational purpose of this critical thinking? It is usually supposed to trigger students' reflection, so that they no longer take for granted their given moral beliefs and commitments since the reflection enables them to make clear what they know and don't know. It allows them to recognize the limitations of their own moral beliefs and to imagine the possibilities beyond them, i.e. other sets of moral beliefs and commitment. In other words, critical thinking enables them to have a distance from what they have believed to be right or wrong, and obtain a more *objective* perspective on it as a whole. As a result, this reflection would allow them to have a sense of autonomy, in the sense that they are now enabled to *will* for themselves a commitment to a certain set of moral ideas and beliefs, including the one handed down from their parents and society *as their own*.

But would it be sufficient to facilitate students' *ownership* of their moral ideas and beliefs for moral teaching? Above all, what does the ownership have to do with our being morally good or virtuous? Before we reflect, we could genuinely find our way around the social world without much trouble by using our moral knowledge on what is right to believe or do. But once we reflect upon it critically, we feel that we should be doing something else. That is, ethical reflection on what we thought is right or wrong becomes part of the practice it considers, and inherently modifies the ethical practice, even our reassured commitment to it. In this sense, ethical reflection may destroy our given moral knowledge. This is why to teach young students to be critical of their moral knowledge is sometimes considered dangerous; it could lead them to get lost in their ethical orientation.[1]

However, according to Williams (1985, p. 168), 'In the process of losing ethical knowledge we may gain knowledge of other kinds, about human nature, history, or what the world is actually like'; in other words, 'we can gain knowledge about, or around, the ethical'. Thus, Williams claims that 'inside the ethical, by the same process, we may gain *understanding*' (1985, p. 168). Despite the ambiguity of what Williams means by 'understanding', I would call the *understanding* (of the ethical) the very aim of Socratic teaching and describe it as a form of *unlearning*, given moral knowledge. And I will show below how Socrates in *the Meno* makes use of critical thinking to lead Meno into the understanding of the ethical, even if he ultimately failed.[2]

While reading Plato's dialog, *the Meno*, we are often puzzled by Socrates as a teacher because his intention in leading the dialog with Meno, a promising young man who is intellectually curious and confident, appears so opaque to us. Socrates' brilliant questionings and rigid arguments look suspicious, as if masking his ulterior motive. In questioning Meno about *what he knows* about what virtue is, Socrates does not mean to seek a theory on the nature of virtue, although his unrelenting interest in the definition of virtue makes us think he does. What Socrates really does is to *critically examine* what Meno knows about what virtue is (Bruell, 1999, p. 169). But, interestingly enough, Socrates' questioning doesn't seem to be geared to helping Meno to find out the right answer, or to persuade him to agree with Socrates himself, or even to encourage Meno to seek his own view on it. Socrates' persistent cross-examination seems rather skillfully designed to frustrate Meno, only to make him realize that he did not know what he thought he knew.

Shown in frustrated Meno's description of Socrates as a torpedo fish that 'makes anyone who comes close and touches it feel numb' (Plato, 1981, pp. 68–69), Socrates deliberately perplexes Meno by questioning and exhausting his answers as all mistaken. Later in the dialog, Socrates indicates his intention in referring to the case of the slave boy:

> Do you think that before he (the slave boy) would have tried to find out that which he thought he knew though he did not, before he fell into perplexity he realized he did not know and longed to know? (p. 73)

That is, Socrates intentionally leads Meno into the state of aporia, only to make him *long to know* since we do not seriously desire to know before we realize our self-ignorance.

However, the difficulty with Socrates' teaching method as critical questioning lies in its possible failure to produce in us longing to know even if we are led into aporia. This was exactly the case with Meno, as shown by numerous textual evidences throughout the dialog.[3] But this failure did not make the intellectually curious and eager Meno stop seeking the answer to his initial question of whether virtue can be taught; he continues to bring up this question and tries to engage Socrates into the question. Meno's single-minded concern with theory-oriented knowledge persists, despite his failure to long to know. This shows that the kind of knowledge involved in 'longing to know' must be distinctive from theory-oriented knowledge in its nature.

Then, we can ask what exactly Meno missed to learn by failing fully to acknowledge his self-ignorance? Or what is the educational function of the acknowledgment of self-ignorance? In describing 'reasonableness' in terms of the acceptance of fallibilism that 'I could be mistaken', Bubules (1995, chapter 7) claims that fallibilism requires us to reflect not only on the fact that 'we have *made* a mistake', but also on the question of 'why it happened and how we can change to avoid repeating it in the future'. If we apply the same requirements to the Socratic acknowledgement of self-ignorance, we may say the followings as to Meno's failure. First, Meno failed to reflect that he made a mistake about a particular fact, i.e. that he did not know what virtue is; this concerns his awareness of a particular fact to be corrected. Secondly, he failed to reflect that what was to be blamed for this mistake was his own habit of mind since it is what forced him to make the mistake; this concerns his awareness of himself as the source of error.

However, I don't think that the acceptance of fallibilism plays the same role as the acknowledgement of self-ignorance does in producing knowledge. The former may lead us to change our mind to have a better opinion, if we are eager to learn. With the acceptance of fallibilism, we are led to realize ourselves as the source of error, only to correct ourselves or not to make the same mistake in the future. On the other hand, with Socratic acknowledgement of self-ignorance as supposedly the best of human wisdom, we are led to see ourselves not just as the source of error, but as self-ignorant in our nature, only to have a more *objective* understanding of ourselves *as* a species. In other words, this understanding tells us that we are a kind of creatures who know that we are self-ignorant; awareness of the human nature as endlessly short of the absolute knowledge, no matter how hard we try. According to Socrates, this self-knowledge as an ignorant species becomes the very source of *our longing to know*, endless desire for knowledge with a love of wisdom. For, this self-knowledge as a philosophical understanding of ourselves is exactly what enables us to see the real possibility of knowing within ourselves.

Thus, the kind of self-knowledge involved in longing to know is not of theory-oriented knowledge that concerns the certainty or betterness of knowledge, but of knowledge in which we are always *present* as knowing subjects, aware of self-limitation as well as self-possibility. As a limit-experience, this is exactly what opens to us the horizon to see *the possibility* of living in the same universe with other human beings who have different moral outlooks. This characteristic of Socratic self-knowledge is essential to what Williams earlier calls 'understanding' or 'being inside the ethical', which can be gained only through the experience of 'losing ethical knowledge'. In this sense, critical thinking as the critical questioning of ethical knowledge can play an educationally important role in bringing students into the experience of 'losing the ethical knowledge' and motivate them to attempt at a new relationship with the given ethical knowledge.[4]

In conclusion, we can say that the critical self-examination in Socratic teaching is not to be directed to moral knowledge (or rationally justifiable positions), but to *reflection* upon one's own moral position or even upon one's relation to the position in his or her life. And this reflection in its character may not necessarily make students virtuous; but it seems to cultivate their inner condition for the *ethical state*, which Williams assumes as the aim of moral education, by leading them to obtain the acknowledgement of self-ignorant as a human species. This inner condition is the very condition that allows us to see the possibility of *living in* the same moral universe with others of different moral outlooks. Hence, we can say that critical thinking in Socratic teaching can be a way of cultivating our students' orientation toward their ethical state.

3. Confucian Teaching for Self-knowledge

3.1. Uneasy Relation Between li *(禮) and* ren *(仁)?*

Confucian moral teaching aims at fostering children to conform to given social norms and values. Modern educators may wonder how it would differ from mere socialization or indoctrination. Wei-ming Tu does not deny that it can be called a process of socialization, but tries to characterize it in a different way. He says:

> In the Confucian perspective a young person involved in the process of socialization is not passively trying to adapt himself or herself to the adult world without being aware of the rules of the game. Children do not socialize themselves and they do not know the mechanism that shaped very dimensions of their lives. But they do participate *actively* in their own socialization by responding *creatively* to their elders' invitations. For they know with increasing sophistication that they are vital to the well-being of the community and that the elders share with them a deep concern for their health growth. (Tu, 1989, p. 36, the italics' being mine)

The above passage suggests two things about the characteristics of Confucian teaching as a process of socialization. First, there is what is to be given *as* normative to young students, namely 'the adult world'. Second, students are encouraged to participate in it 'actively' and 'creatively', not passively to conform to it. This suggests that, even if a fixed set of moral knowledge is supposed to be given or imposed in the Confucian teaching, the manner in which young students are introduced into it does not have to be forceful or authoritarian.

Conformist-looking practice of the Confucian teaching has been subject to harsh criticisms by modern educators in East Asian countries for the reason that it tends to produce young generations as *uncritical* norm-followers or the right answer-obsessed *passive* learners. Wei-ming Tu's different interpretation above makes us wonder if there may be an alternative way of depicting a Confucian learner as a man of 'autonomous obedience' or 'cultured conformity' or even 'self-fulfilling formality'. This is the task I set up for myself in this section.

THE CONFUCIAN CONCEPT OF LEARNING

As the first step to do so, let me first reconstruct the main characteristics of the Confucian teaching? According to Wei-ming Tu, Confucius attempts to teach us to learn to be fully human by 'providing a standard for us in our search for ultimate *personal* knowledge' (1989, p. 29). Tu also adds that 'Confucius taught more by deed than by word'. (1989, p. 36). What is to be noted here is twofold. First, learning to be fully human from the Confucian teaching is continuously and intensely *personal*. Second, the teacher is supposed to inspire students by setting up a standard or being an exemplary figure himself or herself, instead of merely instructing them what to do. Thus, we can say that the Confucian teaching is supposed to help young students pursue their own *personal* knowledge of *tao* (道), the *Way* (self-knowledge), by means of inspiring them to *internalize* given social norms and values.

The internalizing of given social norms and values means learning how to conduct in accordance with *li* (禮), specific rules of proper behaviors that are both practical and ritualistic as social morality. On the other hand, students' *personal* pursuit of *tao* (道), the *Way*, is the process of self-cultivation for the ultimate virtue of Confucian moral character called *ren* (仁), often translated as variously as benevolence, charity, humanity, love, human heartedness, and goodness. What is original about the Confucian philosophy is that it attempts to establish a conceptual connection between two key concepts, *li* (禮) and *ren* (仁), which are potentially in tension while being essential to its philosophy. Thus, it can be formulated as follows: *li* (禮) as social morality is the externalization of *ren* (仁) as personal morality, and *ren* (仁) as personal morality is the personalization or individuation of the formalized social norms *li* (禮). Given this formulation, we wonder now *how* exactly young students' cultivation of *ren* (仁) as the personalization of *li* (禮) can be achieved. The plausibility of an answer to this question may be critical for us to decide on whether the Confucian learning may be in its essence conformist or not.

How are we supposed to cultivate *ren* (仁), then? According to Tu, we need to 'nourish our internal resources and develop a sense of personal direction' and 'this path involves disciplined and daily practice' of *li* (禮) (1989, p. 37) as well as reading classical texts (文) that contain in them the life stories and wisdoms of Confucian sages from the past who practiced *li* (禮). This tells us that the main pedagogical practice for students is twofold: daily practice of *li* (禮) and reading books. And the fact that 'Confucius taught more by deed than by word' also suggests that learning deeds through daily practice of *li* (禮) is more important to learning letters through reading books in the Confucian tradition.

Let me find some textual evidences for this interpretation from the *Analects*[5]:

> The Master said: 'As a young brother and son, be filial (xiao 孝) at home and deferential (di 弟) in the community: be cautious in what you say and then make good on your word (xin 信); love the multitude broadly and be intimate with those who are authoritative in their conduct (ren 仁). If in so behaving you still have energy left, use it to improve yourself through study.' (1:6)

> Zixi said: 'As for persons who care for character much more than beauty, who in serving their parents are able to exert themselves utterly, who give

their whole person in the service of their ruler, and who, in interaction with colleagues and friends, make good on their word (xin 信)—even if it were said of such persons that they are unschooled, I would insist that they are well educated indeed.' (1:7)

The two passages make a clear distinction between one's *good conducts* in relation to parents, others outside home, and what he or she says, on the one hand, and his or her *study* (學文) or *being schooled* (學), on the other hand, while stressing the priority of the former over the latter in education. Here 'study' or 'being schooled' denotes reading books for 'the acquisition and appropriation of the meaning invested in the cultural tradition' (Hall & Ames, 1978, p. 46) by means of a rote memorization of historical and cultural texts of the classics. It seems clear here that the ultimate aim of learning to read books is to learn how to conduct in relation to others and to one's words; and we can even claim that learning to read books in itself may be educationally trivial unless it contributes to the cultivation of one's moral virtues, *especially* social virtues in relation to others.

Here we can see that being learned in the Confucian sense is always defined in terms of others-concerned social morality. Its primary emphasis on deeds and conducts in relation to others may be even suspected as anti-intellectualist. But what follows below makes us suspend this suspicion:

The Master said: 'There are, in a town of ten households, bound to be people who are better than I am in doing their utmost (zhōng 忠) and in making good on heir word (xin 信), but there will be no one who can compare with me in the love of learning.' (5:28)

Duke Ai inquired, 'Which of your disciples truly loves learning (haoxue 好學)?'

Confucius replied, 'There was one Yan Hui who truly loved learning. He did not take his anger out on others; he did not make the same mistake twice. Unfortunately, he was to die young. Nowadays, there is no one—at least, I haven't come across anyone—who truly loves learning.' (6:3)

There are two things to be noticed from the passages above. First, Confucius deplores over the fact that, even if it is not rare to meet those who are excellent at their conducts, it is very rare to meet those who are eager to learn *as well as* being excellent at their conduct. It implies how difficult it is to seek the cultivation of one's moral virtue *ren* (仁) through *both* good conduct (in relation to others) and good learning (of culture for oneself). Second, Confucius still quite strongly emphasizes the value of learning for oneself, expressed in 'loving to learn', in the pursuit of moral virtue *ren* (仁). Despite his modesty, Confucius unabashedly prides himself on his eagerness to learn and further describes his favorite disciple, Yan Hui, in similar terms. This tells us that one's *enthusiasm for* learning itself is one of Confucius' primary concerns in his teaching.

In making a distinction between good conduct (in relation to others) and good learning for oneself, Confucius certainly shows that his ethics of learning is not all about the *mere delivery* of others-concerned social morality; there is an additional qualification to be met. On the other hand, even if Confucius places his priority upon good conduct over reading books or being schooled, there is no doubt that he believes that learning of traditional culture (學文) is a necessary condition for the *effective* development of a moral person. However, in what sense is the literary education considered to be effective for the cultivation of our moral virtue? In other words, what is the pedagogical status of learning culture or reading books in the Confucian philosophy of education? We may find a clue for an answer from the above passage. Confucius seems to look down a bit upon the ordinary villagers for mere good conduct of theirs, despite the fact that he values good conduct more highly than reading books for his teaching in general. Why is that so? It is because they lack a passion for learning to be fully human. Thus, we can speculate that the pedagogical value of reading books for Confucius may lie in its role of triggering our passion for (moral) learning.

How can reading books trigger our desire for moral learning to be virtuous? Is it always the case? We know very well that being knowledgeable is one thing and being virtuous is another thing. According to Keum-Joong Hwang (2010, p. 255), in the Confucian tradition, reading books about the life examples of Confucian sages trigger us to *think* and *reflect* as a moral stimulus since they are the records of the sages' self-experiential reflections on their lives for their self-cultivation. Thus, reading classical texts is likely to lead us to reflect on our own conduct with an awakened passion for moral learning. Of course, we can also *reflect* on our conduct without necessarily reading books or studying. In fact, the daily practice of *li* (禮) itself can trigger us to reflect on our conduct, if we are attentive as well as eager enough to learn from our own experiences.[6] But it is rare to take place, as shown in Confucius' description of the good ordinary villagers. Thus, reading books can be a good pedagogical guide that awakens our reflection as well as our desire for moral learning. What is to be noted here is that our reflection and our eagerness to learn seem to go hand in hand.

In conclusion, we may say that in the Confucian education, what qualifies someone's good conduct *as* good conduct is not mere good conduct, but good conduct *with* some reflection accompanied by it on the part of the agent. Without reflection accompanied, good conduct is likely to remain formalistic and conformist, susceptible to criticism of social adjustment to the status quo. Thus, we can say that what makes our self-cultivation of *ren* (仁) antiseptic of cultural and political conformism is the activity of reflection or thinking, which in fact constitutes an essential part in the process of self-cultivation.

3.2. *Reflection* (思) *as a Way to* enliven *given moral knowledge*

Against Weber's thesis that 'Confucian rationalism meant rational adjustment to the world', Wei-ming Tu claims that the thesis can be correct 'only if one bears in mind that "adjustment" does not mean compliance to the status quo'. For him, 'a Confucianist may very well refute an established *li* (禮) by exposing its incomparability with *ren* (仁)' (Tu, 1979, p. 12). And he concludes that the tension between *li* (禮) and *ren* (仁) can be characterized as a *creative* tension. He says:

To use Harvey Cox's analogy, *li* means the standards of this world, whereas *ren* means the summons to choice and answerability. *Li* signifies the fact that a man lives in society; *ren* points to the equally important fact that he is more than the intersection of social forces ... Man cannot live without *li*, but when *li* becomes wholly determinative, he is no longer really man. In a deeper sense, therefore the creative tension between *ren* and *li* suggests a kind of interdependence. As a result, the Confucian philosophers acknowledge the coercive nature of society not only passively as a given condition, but also positively as a creative instrumentality. (1979, p. 13)

From the passage, we can notice that Tu sees through a possible discrepancy between *li* (禮) as social norms and *ren* (仁) as a personal virtue in the Confucian moral universe, and suggests how the idea of *ren* can play a role of preventing Confucianists from being sheer conventionalists, although culturally conservative. Thus, to spell out, the role of reflection or thinking in the process of self-cultivation of *ren* (仁) will be a good way of supporting Tu's interpretation above.

How can we describe the nature of 'reflection' in the Confucian learning? How different would it be from critical thinking discussed earlier in the Socratic teaching? To get closer to a plausible answer to these questions, let me start with two very famous sayings from the *Analects*:

The master said: 'learning without due reflection leads to perplexity: reflection without learning leads to perilous circumstances.' (2:15)

Master Zeng said: 'Daily I examine my person on three counts. In my undertakings on behalf of other people, have I failed to do my utmost (zhong, 忠). In my interaction with colleagues and friends, have I failed to make good on my word (xin, 信)? In what has been passed on to me, have I failed to carry it into practice?' (1:4)

The 'learning' mentioned in the first passage can mean 'learning through either practicing *li* (禮) or reading books', as discussed earlier. We can easily understand that if we practice *li* (禮) without reflection, that is practicing *li* (禮) just because we are told for it to be right, and we read books mechanically, it would make us feel lost at a certain point of our lives about the point of what we are doing. Without any care about what we are doing, it would be very hard for us to be meaningfully engaged in what we are doing for self-cultivation.

On the other hand, if we just keep reflecting upon *li* (禮) without learning, i.e. without practicing *li* (禮) or reading books about it, our reflection would not have any specific contents to deal with. It would be empty or dangerous because it is not grounded on our living reality or our sense of life. Without learning, our reflection on the moral knowledge of *li* (禮) would not bring about any practical consequences upon our conduct, remaining as a string of obscure, fuzzy, and airy ideas. Without learning, our reflection on the moral knowledge of *li* (禮) could make us dogmatic in defense of some political ideology.

Then, what kind of reflection is required for our Confucian self-cultivation? As well specified in the second passage above, our Confucian reflection does not concern the *objective* meanings or significances of *li* (禮); the latter is already taken for granted. Our reflection is supposed to pay attention to *the way* we practice *li* (禮) or the manner in which we commit ourselves to the particular *li* (禮) as a given moral knowledge. We may reformulate Master Zeng's self-examination in the following questions: 'Have I done enough to live up to the principle and spirit of the *li* (禮) concerned? or "Have I taken the right action with the *right heart-mind*?" for the *li* (禮) demanded by the situation?' I think this is a kind of reflection that tends to be motivated by our strong desire to be good or virtuous.

David Hall and Roger Ames hold that in Confucian vision, learning is not so much about the acquisition of 'a conceptually mediated knowledge of a world of objective fact' as about 'an unmediated process of *becoming aware*'. And they also claim that 'thinking (思) for Confucius is not to be understood as a process of abstract reasoning, but is fundamentally performative in that it is an activity whose immediate consequences is the achievement of a practical result' (1978, p. 44). Their descriptions of learning as a form of 'becoming aware' and of reflection as basically practical, not theoretical, may remind us of a form of self-cultivation in pursuit of *phronesis* or practical wisdom in the Aristotelian sense, wisdom that tells us what to choose as the right thing to do at the right time.

However, Herbert Fingarette claims (Fingarette, 1972, p. 22) that thinking (思) in Confucian learning is not a matter of *deliberation* among the equally valid alternatives of actions to get a practical wisdom, as in the case with the Aristotelian ethics. For example, when the Master said: "There is nothing I can do for someone who is not constantly asking himself: 'What to do? What to do?'" (15:16), Fingarette holds that the concern that the Confucian disciple seems to have here is not with choice. The phrase 'What to do? What to do?' does not need to be read as 'What about this alternative, should I do it or not?' Instead, according to Fingarette, we should suppose that there is presumed to be only one right thing to do. And the question at stake is then in fact: "What about this?, is it right? Is it the Way (*tao*, 道)?" The task here, in Fingarette's view, is not about making a choice but about making 'the attempt to *characterize* some object of action as *objectively* right or not' (1972, p. 22, the italics' being mine); 'The moral task is to make a proper classification, to locate an act within the scheme of *li*.' (p. 22).

Fingarette gives us another example that can support the same view on the nature of thinking (思) in the Confucian moral vision. He makes a comment on the following saying of Confucius':

> Zizhang inquired about accumulating excellence (de 德) and sorting things out when in a quandary. The Master replied, "to take doing one's utmost (zhong 忠), making good on one's word (xin 信), and seeking out what is appropriate (yi 義) as one's main concerns, is to accumulate excellence. To simultaneously love and hate someone, and thus to simultaneously want this person to love and to die, is to be in quandary. 'You surely do not gain fortune this way; you only get something different'." (12:10)

Here the mind deluded or in error is not the mind in doubt as to which course to choose, but the mind of a person being inconsistent in his or her desires or acts. The task of the mind here in thinking is not a matter of choosing or deciding, but of distinguishing or discriminating the inconsistent inclinations within oneself, according to Fingarette. In other words, the task of Confucian mind can be posed in terms of knowing as being aware, rather than choosing. Thus, we can say that learning in the Confucian sense is not concerned with deliberation for a choice, but with recognition.

How can we then reach this recognition and be assured of its being objectively right? Fingarette says that it is our moral task to try to discover which would be the true path and to detect 'which is only an apparent path, perhaps a clearing in the brush leading nowhere except into brambles'. In order to be able to do so, 'we need only make a tacit assumption that there *is tao* (道), a Way, a self-consistent, self-authenticating way of universal scope' without any slightest doubt (1972, p. 24). In other words, what is required for our learning in Confucian moral universe is to take a tacit assumption that there exists *tao* (道) as the source of the truth of *li* (禮), and to unconditionally follow *li* (禮) as the objective moral knowledge. *Tao* (道), the Way, as the underlying principle of *li*, is considered recognizable, invisible though, by everyone if he or she is well attuned to his or her inner nature.

Thus, the Confucian sense of learning (學) in the form of 'becoming aware' can be said to refer to one's personal awareness of *dao* (道) by way of getting to know how to live in accordance with *li* (禮) in his or her everyday life. And reflection (思) can be attributed to this ordeal of the Confucian learning as a long existential journey in pursuit of one's own *dao* (道). This journey involves in the task of *characterizing* some object of action as *objectively* right or not in one's practice of *li* (禮). There are two main characteristics about the nature of reflection implied here. First, in reflecting, we always assume that there is the *objectively right* answer, and that *li* (禮) is the right set of the rules of our conduct. Thus, our absolute obedience to *li* (禮) as social norms is required for learning. Second, thinking (思) in the Confucian vision is not mobilized to *prove* that some act is objectively right or to justify *why li* (禮) is the right rites to follow, but it is just to *characterize* the (given) act as the *right* act or the given *li* (禮) as the right *li* (禮). Assuming there is the objectively right version of answer, our Confucian reflection engages in how to *characterize* or *make sense* of the (given) act as the right act *through* our own practice and life experiences.

This process of characterizing or making-sensing seems to be achieved *only by* living out the act as the right act in one's own everyday life, diligently and ceaselessly and with one's whole being involved, cognitive, emotional, bodily, and cultural. In this sense, the activity of characterization is a long self-experiential and even existential inner struggle. Living out some acts in this manner can be said to be a way of creating one's own meanings of the acts as right; we create the meanings of the acts for ourselves, either by repeatedly practicing them with reflection, or by referring to the classical texts which are full of Confucian sages' self-experiential interpretations of *li* (禮). This means that, without living out the acts or knowledge, there will be no meanings of our acts and knowledge created, and without no meanings created, there will be no learning for us. Here we can see that in the Confucian moral universe, learning is inseparable with living.

If living in accordance to *li* (禮) is always accompanied by the meaning-attributing activity of reflection, it would make everyday life of a Confucian learner very lively and active. In fact, they live their lives endowed with rich meanings in practicing *li* (禮) in relation to others. This learning by living with reflection can be described as the very way of *unlearning* the moral knowledge of *li* (禮). And the accumulation of this process of unlearning would bring us self-knowledge in the form of our personal knowledge of *dao* (道); one knows how he or she is connected to the Confucian moral universe with his or her place in it. This self-knowledge is what makes us be *ren* (仁), good and virtuous.

However, what should be noted here is that there is no way in which we can prove that our own discovery of *dao* (道) as self-knowledge or the meaning created by it would be *objectively* right or not; the objectivity of *dao* (道) does not seem to be anybody's concern in the Confucian teaching. *Tao* (道), as accessible only by one's personal knowledge in the Confucian moral universe, plays a role of a good inner source that would lead us to conduct well in actualizing *li* (禮) with its richer moral meanings. As long as it plays this role well, so that we know how to conduct and live well in accordance with *li* (禮) with fuller meanings, the question about the objectivity of *dao* (道) does not occur; our lives and acts are the very places where *dao* (道) and its moral meanings reside in, according to the Confucian teaching. Thus, we can also say that *dao* (道) as one's personal knowledge is the criterion for the workability and practicality of *li* (禮), not the other way around. For, it is the very source that endows *li* (禮) with moral meanings.

4. Conclusion: Two Different Forms of Thinking, Two Different Forms of Humanness

I have attempted to examine and reconstruct two different senses of self-knowledge as two distinct forms of *ethical* knowledge advocated by Socratic and Confucian teachings. This attempt is made as a way of calling into question some common misunderstandings in our educational thinking, frequently derived from the stereotyped comparisons between the Socratic self and the Confucian self, such as an intellectualist vs. a moralist, an active learner vs. a passive learner, and an anti-traditionalist vs. pro-traditionalist. Here my discussion tends to focus on the role of thinking in the acquisition of self-knowledge, especially how it helps us *unlearn* the moral knowledge we have already acquired; the process of unlearning is the very process in which our ethical state of being is transformed.

Socratic teaching makes use of critical thinking to encourage young students *to unlearn* their given moral knowledge by *shocking* them *into* intellectual and psychological numbness, which will redirect them to *newly establish* their (personal) relation to the earlier moral knowledge. In other words, self-knowledge always comes after a sense of disconcertment or disorientation, which is supposed to make learners have a perspective on how they stand in relation to their moral knowledge. This perspective affects the way they are, if not necessarily makes them good or virtuous; but it psychologically and intellectually prepares them for being good or virtuous.

On the other hand, Confucian teaching starts with a tacit assumption that tradition and its given social norms have an absolute authority not to be doubted. This assumption seems to define the nature and function of 'reflection' in the Confucian learning. Reflection is involved and mobilized to help students characterize and make sense of their moral knowledge of *li* (禮) *as* the right one. It helps them *personalize* the moral knowledge by making them *inhabit* the knowledge or by *acting on* it repeatedly in their everyday practice. In other words, reflection helps them *unlearn* the given moral knowledge by enabling them to become aware of what it means *for them* to experience or live out the knowledge in their own lives. Learning given moral knowledge is living it out *in one's own manner*, and reflection mediates between learning and living in this process. Thus, reflection brings to the students self-knowledge as their personal way of enlivening the given knowledge, and, in this sense, self-knowledge in Confucian vision is exactly what makes them become good or virtuous.

The activity of thinking in whatever form requires by its nature its agents, their active and voluntary engagement. Once it is activated, it tends to create new knowledge for the agents. Then, what motivates us to think in the first place? This is one of the biggest educational mysteries. Both traditions of teaching seem to tell us that we humans are born with the mind, so that a tendency to think is human nature. The way each tradition gives us an account of how we are motivated to think is quite different. 'Critical thinking' in Socratic teaching is likely to be developed when students are asked to give reasons for their actions or the meanings of their words. 'Reflection' in the Confucian teaching tends to be awakened when students take seriously and are fully committed to what is given to them. If we think in a different manner, we become a different kind of human being. So, if we have two different traditions of thinking, it can be said that we have inherited two different ways of developing humanness in us.

The late-modern condition in which we now live does not allow us to believe in the idea of inborn human nature. And the humanities as we now know of turn out to have cultural foundations, but culture is also man-made. This brings us into a conclusion that two different forms of humanness is to be equally developed and respected side by side, probably in such a way as to produce a new kind of humanness, by making the two cultures compatible in our educational settings. This conclusion also suggests how weighty our responsibility as teachers may be in the ever-globalizing transcultural world today, especially in regard to the ever soul-searching question of what it means to be human *to* us, inheritors of both traditions.

Disclosure statement

No potential conflict of interest was reported by the author.

Funding

This work was supported by the National Research Foundation of Korea [grant number 2014S1A5A2A01014800].

Notes

1. Here I use the terms 'moral' and 'ethical' interchangeably, taking them in a broad sense that includes obligations and duties as well as virtues.

2. The discussion below is excerpted from my earlier essay entitled 'Critical thinking, Education, and Post-modernity' (Kwak, 2008) and reconstructed in such a way to fit the current argument. For the detailed argument, you can refer to the essay.
3. See the text at 82a (1981, p. 70) and 86d (p. 76).
4. Hannah Arendt describes in her last book *The Life of the Mind* (Arendt, 1971, p. 189) this kind of self-examination as one's being a friend with oneself in the form of self-dialog.
5. The citations from the *Analects* in this paper are all from the version translated by Ames and Rosemont (1998, New York: The Random House Publishing Group).
6. This is true, given Confucius' belief that by nature men are all alike (17:2), and that by nature all men are able to learn (15:39). Here, what seems to enable everyone to learn is one's ability to reflect or think. This is why Confucius *in principle* places his priority on good conduct over reading books or studying.

References

Ames, R. T., & Rosemont H. (1998). trans. *The analects of Confucius: A philosophical translation*, New York, NY: The Random House Publishing Group.
Arendt, H. (1971). *The life of the mind*. New York, NY: A Harvest Book.
Blumenberg, H. (1983). *The legitimacy of the modern age*. (R. M. Wallace, Trans.). Cambridge, MA: The MIT Press.
Bruell, C. (1999). *On the Socratic education*. New York, NY: Rowman & Littlefield.
Bubules, N. (1995). Reasonable doubt. In W. Kohli (Ed.), *Critical conversations in philosophy of education*. New York, NY: Routledge.
Fingarette, H. (1972). *Confucius: The secular as sacred*. New York, NY: Harper Torch Books.
Hall, D. L., & Ames, R. T. (1978). *Thinking through Confucius*. Albany: State University of New York Press.
Hwang, K.-J. (2010). 'Reading' as 'Gewuzhizhigongfu' in Zhu xi's philosophy of Gongfu. *The Korean Journal of Philosophy of Education*, 47, 249–280.
Kwak, D.-J. (2008). Critical thinking, education, and post-modernity. *Asia Pacific Education Review*, 9, 127–135.
Li, J. (2012). *Cultural foundations of learning*. Cambridge: Cambridge University Press.
Nussbaum, M. C. (1997). *Cultivating humanity: A classical defense of reform in liberal education*. Cambridge, MA: Harvard University Press.
Nussbaum, M. C. (2010). *Not for profit: Why democracy needs the humanities*. Princeton: Princeton University Press.
Peters, M. (2015). Socrates and Confucius: The cultural foundations and ethics of learning, *Educational Philosophy of Theory*, 47, 423–427.
Plato. (1981). *Five dialogues: Euthyphro, apology, crito, meno, phaedo* (1st ed.). (G. M. A. Grube, Trans.). Indianapolis, IN: Hackett Publishing Company.
Tu, W.-m. (1979). *Humanity and self-cultivation: Essays on Confucian thought*. Berkeley: Asian Humanities Press.

Tu, W.-m. (1989), *Way, learning and politics: Essays on the confucian intellectual*. Cambridge, MA: The Institute of East Asian Philosophies.

Williams, B. (1985). *Ethics and the limits of philosophy*. Cambridge, MA: Harvard University Press.

Yu, J. (2005). The beginning of ethics: Confucius and Socrates. *Asian Philosophy, 15*, 173–189.

Humanistic Traditions, East and West: Convergence and divergence

MORIMICHI KATO

Abstract

The term 'humanism' is Western in origin. It denotes the tradition that places special emphasis on cultivation of letters for education. In the West, this tradition was originated with sophists and Isocrates, established by Cicero, and was developed by Renaissance humanists. East Asia, however, also has its own humanistic traditions with equal educational relevance. One of these is a Japanese version of Confucian humanism established by Ogyu Sorai (1666–1728). This tradition is based on the interpretation of Confucius as a lover of poetry and a teacher of rites. In this article, we discuss the main features of East Asian humanism represented by Sorai and Confucius. Then, after an overview of Western humanism, we aim to elucidate both the convergence and divergence of the two traditions. The investigation will help us (hopefully) to envision humanistic education of the twenty-first century.

Introduction

This article intends to compare the humanistic traditions that have played significant roles in the culture and education of the East and the West. The comparison will elucidate not only common features but also significant differences.

We use the term 'humanism' for the tradition that places special emphasis on cultivation of letters for education. Humanistic tradition in the West had its roots in ancient Greece and Rome. It flourished during the Renaissance and influenced the modern educational theories of Bildung and liberal arts.

The humanistic traditions of East Asia, however, have been largely neglected by scholars of humanism and historians of education. This is surprising, given that typically humanistic features such as philological study of ancient texts, imitation of ancient literature, and a profound love of letters are found throughout East Asia.

Our scope in investigating this vast ocean of East Asian humanism is a humble one. We focus on a Japanese version of Confucian humanistic tradition represented by Ogyu Sorai (1666–1728). The merit of this selection is that it presents certain features that can be fruitfully compared to those of Western humanistic traditions. Sorai is a fascinating figure. He not only provided his own humanistic interpretation of Confucius, but also exerted a great influence on the humanistic studies of Japanese literature. In this sense, he can be regarded as a founder of Japanese humanism (Kato, 2014a).

Sorai and the Humanistic Interpretation of Confucius

Sorai was originally a follower of Zhu Xi philosophy. Zhu Xi philosophy was developed by Cheng Yi, Cheng Hao, and Zhu Xi in the Song dynasty (960–1279). It is characterized by a grandiose theory that comprises metaphysics, cosmology, politics, and ethics. In Japan, it became the official doctrine of the Tokugawa shogunate. However, by the seventeenth century, major thinkers raised their voices against Zhu Xi philosophy, such as Nakae Toju (1608–1648) and Ito Jinsai (1627–1705).

The turning point of Sorai's intellectual life occurred when, at the age of 39, he bought a collection of books imported from China, in which he found the books of Li P'an-lung (1514–1570) and Wang Shih-chen (1526–1590) (Lidin, 1973, pp. 99–100).

Both Li and Wang were prominent scholars of the school of ancient rhetoric, which was developed in China in the sixteenth century (Yoshikawa, 1975, pp. 118–172). As the name indicates, this school of rhetoric encouraged imitation of classical Chinese poets. What is remarkable about Sorai's reception of ancient rhetoric was that he used his knowledge of ancient literature primarily as a tool for interpretation rather than of composition. Gadamer once remarked on the special link between rhetoric (art of composition) and hermeneutics (art of interpretation) (Gadamer, 1975, p. 177). For him, hermeneutics is a kind of reversal (*Umkehrung*) of rhetoric and poetics. For example, understanding the techniques for composing poetry can aid in the interpretation of poetry. This is the reason why the hermeneutics of the modern West was influenced by rhetoric.

Something similar happened with Sorai. The works of Li and Wang, which recommended using ancient words, contained many words that Sorai could not understand. So he made a vow that he would read only ancient literature written before the Western Han period (206 BC–9 AD), notably the Six Classics (the *Book of Poetry*, the *Book of History*, the *Book of Rites*, the *Book of Music*, the *Book of Changes*, and the *Spring and Autumn Annals*). This study, he confessed, was extremely difficult, because the study of the Confucian texts in his time was mainly centered on the Four Books (the *Analects*, the *Mencius*, the *Great Learning*, and the *Doctrine of the Mean*) that were, with the exception of the *Analects*, of a later age. The language of the Six Classics, especially of the *Book of Poetry*, is of a much earlier era and thus required great effort to understand. Sorai said later that he had to read them repeatedly until the meaning of words was revealed through their contexts (Lidin, 1973, pp. 99–100).

Through the study of the Six Classics, Sorai acquired a historical sense of language and began to notice a great deficiency in later Confucianism: it tended to assume a universal, timeless point of view, and thus had no sense of history. To quote Sorai,

> They [the Cheng Brothers and Zhu Xi] did not realize that the contemporary language of their day was not the same as that of ancient sages, nor did

they realize that contemporary literature was not the same as that of the ancients. (Sorai, 2006, p. 172)

This deficiency had devastating effects when later Confucians attempted to interpret older texts. Lacking sufficient knowledge of language and history, they interpreted them from the perspective of the later system of Zhu Xi philosophy, thus completely missing the sense of the original text. In his main work, *Benmei*, Sorai attempts to retrieve the original sense of the central Confucian vocabularies, such as Way, Virtue, Humanity, Wisdom, Sacred, Ritual Propriety, Heaven, and Nature, by applying the method of philology that he acquired through his reading of ancient books.

All this had a tremendous effect upon the interpretation of the *Analects*. Interpreting the first sentence of the *Analects* 1, which begins with the verb 'learn,' Sorai asserts that the object of learning is the Six Classics. Confucius is thus presented as a zealous student of the way of the early kings reflected in the Six Classics (Koyasu, 2008, p. 48). Sorai argued the following:

> 'Learning' refers to studying the way of the early kings. The early kings' way consists of the poems of the *Book of Poetry*, the prose of the *Book of History*, the rites of the *Book of Rites*, and the music of the *Book of Music*. The method of learning therefore should consist in studying what is in the *Book of Poetry*, *Book of History*, *Book of Rites*, and *Book of Music*, and that is all. (Sorai, 2006, pp. 312–313)

This interpretation contrasts with the interpretation of later Confucians, who placed the *Analects* together with the *Mencius*, the *Great Learning*, and the *Doctrine of the Mean*. These Four Books were canonized and made the main subjects of the official examination.

Characteristic of the Four Books (with the notable exception of the *Analects*) is that they develop metaphysical speculation of concepts such as Heaven and Nature. These concepts were important for Confucius himself. And yet, not much discussion is found about them in the *Analects*. In the other three books, we find more detailed treatment of these concepts. The *Doctrine of the Mean*, in particular, is rich in metaphysical speculation. The development of these concepts was then taken over by the Confucians of the Song dynasty. Zhu Xi particularly succeeded in synthesizing them into a unified system.

Sorai, however, opposed this tendency. He could not tolerate later Confucians attributing their metaphysical thought to Confucius. Sorai considered the later metaphysical development of Confucianism as an outcome of the polemic that it had experienced with Buddhism and Taoism (Maruyama, 1974, pp. 77–78; Yoshikawa, 1975, p. 83, pp. 129–131). It was, for him, simply a deviation from the original sense of the *Analects*.

We have examined how the philology that Sorai learned through the study of the Six Classics led to his interpretation of Confucianism. It was quite revolutionary in a time dominated by Zhu Xi philosophy.

Let us now turn to Confucius and examine the relevance of Sorai's interpretation.

THE CONFUCIAN CONCEPT OF LEARNING

Confucius and humanistic heritage

Confucius' son, Boyu, said that his father gave him no secret doctrine. He only asked him if he learned the Songs [or Poetry] and the rites (*Analects*, 16, 13; cf. 17, 10). This testimony shows the importance of these two books for the Confucian curricula. In *Analects* 8, we find a similar educational program.

These passages show that poetry (songs), rites, and music occupied the core of the Confucian curriculum. According to Morohashi, these three subjects were always combined in the curriculum of that time, since, in the practice of rites, the songs were sung with music (Morohashi, 1973, p. 170).

Many passages in the *Analects* attest to Confucius' predilection for the Songs (for example, *Analects* 2, 2; 3, 20) and music (*Analects* 3, 23; 3, 25; 7, 14; 7, 32). He tried to apply correct original pronunciation to the reading of the Songs (*Analects* 7, 18). He also acknowledged that after returning to Lu, his home country, he had set music right by assigning proper places to the sections of the Songs (*Analects* 9, 15).

Confucius' school was a learning community of friends who together tried to attain the highest humanity through the learning of ancient books and music (*Analects* 1, 1). His faith in ancient books was such that he declined any originality of his own teaching (*Analects* 7, 1). He said, 'I am not the kind of person who has gained knowledge through some natural propensity for it. Rather, loving antiquity, I am earnest in seeking it out.' (*Analects* 7, 20) [The translation of the *Analects* is, when not specified, taken from Ames and Rosemont (1998) with occasional modifications.]

Confucius saw many merits in learning the Songs. He said:

> My young friends, why don't any of you study the Songs? Reciting the Songs can arouse your sensibilities, strengthen your powers of observation, enhance your ability to get on with others, and sharpen your critical skills. Close at hand, it enables you to serve your father, and away at court it enables you to serve your lord. It instills in you a broad vocabulary for making distinctions in the world around you. (*Analects* 17, 9)

For Confucius, the purpose of learning poetry was not primarily esthetic. Rather, it was moral and political. Confucius said,

> If people can recite all of the three hundred Songs and yet when given official responsibility, fail to perform effectively, or when sent to distant quarters, are unable to act on their own initiative, then even though they have mastered so many of them, what good are they to them? (*Analects* 13, 5)

As for metaphysical speculation, Confucius carefully avoided discussions about themes such as human nature and Heaven (*tian*). One of his disciples, Zigong, said, 'We can learn from the Master's cultural refinements, but do not hear him discourse on subjects such as our natural disposition and the way of *tian*' (*Analects*, 5, 13).

This overview of Sorai and Confucius shows us the lineage from Confucius to Sorai. This lineage is characterized by the central role of literature in education.

This does not mean, of course, that the interpretation of Confucius suggested here is the only 'right' one. The lineage that leads from Confucius to Sorai is just one of many lines that bind Confucius with our time.

And yet, this lineage deserves attention from an educational perspective: it created the Confucian humanistic heritage that accorded the study of literature the central role of education. When I call this heritage 'humanistic,' I have in mind the Western heritage of humanism. Indeed, both heritages have much in common. It is, therefore, important to compare both heritages and examine their points of convergence as well as of divergence.

What is the Western Humanistic Tradition?

The term 'humanism' acquired a variety of meanings in the course of history. In the history of educational thought, this term was first used in the nineteenth century Germany to designate the Renaissance educational and artistic movement (Voigt, 1960). The reason behind this naming was that Renaissance teachers of the Greek and Latin were called *umanista*, because they taught *studia humanitatis*, the humanistic studies, such as literature and history (Kristeller, 1955, p. 9). The term *studia humanitatis* can be literally translated as the 'studies of humanity.' But this translation requires specification.

Cicero (106–43 B.C.E.), a Roman orator, translated the Greek term *paideia* into *humanitas*. Thus, *humanitas* had a strong educational connotation. But it also retained the meaning that came from *homo*: the significance of human nature. Besides these two meanings, Cicero sometimes used the term in the sense of social affability (Leeman & Pinkster, 1981, p. 81). Thus, for Cicero, a man of *humanitas* was one who had attained the highest degree of education and was open to conversing with people. In a dialog named *On Orator*, he depicted a Roman orator, Crassus, as a personification of this ideal. Such a man was also one who had fully realized his human nature, because for Cicero the ability to use language was the central feature that distinguished man from beasts. This characteristic of man as a speaking animal was a heritage that Cicero inherited from Isocrates (436–338 B.C.E), a Greek orator and a rival of Plato (429–347 B.C.E.). Isocrates, on the other hand, studied rhetoric under Gorgias (c.485–c.380 B.C.E.), a famous sophist. Thus, a line that begins from the sophists reaches Cicero through Isocrates. This is the tradition of ancient rhetoric (Marrou, 1981).

This tradition played a decisive role in the formation of Renaissance humanism. Petrarch (1304–1374), who can be called the founder of this movement, found books of Cicero in his father's library when he was a small boy. Even though he could not understand Latin, he was fascinated by the beautiful sound of Ciceronian style (Kondo, 1984, p. 26). This experience, recounted by Petrarch in his old age, is symbolic. Against the will of his father, who wanted his son to become a lawyer, Petrarch dedicated his life to the rediscovery of ancient Latin literature. He also became a famous writer. Even though he is now known for his beautiful Italian sonnets, Petrarch's pride lay in his composition of Latin prose and poetry. Petrarch also edited a work by Livy, a Roman historian, who wrote a monumental history of the Roman people. Petrarch collected volumes of this book, which were distributed and hidden in places such as monasteries. These volumes contained many mistakes and came in multiple versions, so he was compelled to examine the language of each text carefully and to compare them meticulously. This led to his understanding of the historical aspect of language. It is through such experiences with ancient texts that philology emerged in the Renaissance.

Petrarch was a passionate seeker of ancient books. Wherever he went, he visited libraries and monasteries to search for them. His followers imitated this activity, and in the beginning of the fifteenth century, there were remarkable new discoveries of ancient books. Among them, the most important was the complete text of Cicero's *On Orator*, discovered in 1421 (Grendler, 1989, p. 120). The book played a decisive role in the formation of Renaissance humanism.

For example, a comparison between this Ciceronian text and *On the Study of Literature* (1424), an educational treatise written by renowned Florentine humanist Leonardo Bruni (1370–1444), shows that Bruni's ideal of an educated person was strongly influenced by the Ciceronian ideal of an educated orator (Kato, 1992). In *On Orator*, an educated orator is depicted as a person whose eloquence is based on a wide knowledge of subjects such as history, ethics, rhetoric, and poetry.

Especially important here is that Bruni, as well as other humanists, stressed the educational value of poetry. At the time when they set this proposal, education was under the strong influence of Scholasticism. Ancient pagan poetry, which often depicted erotic adventures of pagan gods, was banned from the classroom, as it was considered un-Christian and immoral. The humanists of the fifteenth century had to pursue heated debates with the Scholastic scholars to defend the value of pagan poetry in education (Garin, 1975, pp. 23–44). In the same period, new schools were built by famous humanistic teachers such as Guarino da Verona (1374–1460) (Grendler, 1989, pp. 125–141). In these schools, the study of classical literature, including poetry, took a central role. It is through this educational reform of the fifteenth century that the humanistic studies (poetry, history, ethics, and rhetoric written in Latin and Greek) became the core curriculum of secondary education. This influence persists today under the name of liberal education, even though the study of Latin and Greek is becoming obsolete.

Thus, the educational heritage of the West spans ancient rhetoric through Renaissance humanism to the liberal education of our age (Kimball, 1986).

These brief overviews of the humanistic traditions of East and West suggest a certain affinity between them. And yet, it appears that the link between the Confucian and Western humanistic traditions has been almost completely overlooked by scholars. (Previous references to 'Confucian humanism' were based on the idea of the unity of man and Heaven (Chang, 1969, p. 3, p. 15) and the concept of *jen* (translated as 'humanity') (Tu, 1993, pp. 1–12). This is completely different from the humanistic tradition I am trying to elucidate.) And yet, investigation of such a link can be fruitful for three reasons.

First, it can illuminate aspects of the Confucian tradition that can be easily overlooked under a philosophical approach.

Second, it can elevate the ideal of humanism as a common ideal of East and West.

Third, the divergence that can still be found between both traditions can help us understand the differences between them. Such understanding, in turn, can lead us to revise the concept of liberal education that dominates the Western version today.

Let us therefore start investigating this link.

Common features

Three features are common to both traditions, and are of equal importance. We will treat the first two features briefly, since they have already been discussed.

The first feature is the importance of literature (especially poetry) in education: in both cultures, literature is considered the fundamental pillar of moral and political instruction. However, not just any literature would serve this purpose. Both traditions esteemed exemplary ancient literature. For Confucius and Sorai, such works included the writings that supposedly came from the Zhu dynasty, such as the *Book of Poetry*. For Western humanism, it was the classical literature of ancient Rome and Greece. Both traditions also saw the educational value of literature in forming morally upright and politically competent citizens. They did not see literature as an object of leisure or esthetic contemplation.

The second feature common to both traditions is the sense of history nourished by the linguistic study of ancient books. This sense of history was supported by the powerful tool of philology which led them to criticize the dominant theories of their time, Zhu Xi philosophy and Scholasticism, as these neglected a sense of history almost completely.

The third common feature concerns the method of learning. Both Confucian and humanistic traditions provide us with a valuable perspective from which to view modern education.

The fundamental feature of modern education is the pride of having finally found the right method. Pestalozzi, the Swiss educator, notably called his own method *die Methode* (the method), the implication of which is that previous educators lacked the right method.

This obsession with method is not an idiosyncrasy of Pestalozzi. It was Descartes who, in his *Discourse of the Method*, rebuked previous thinkers for their lack of method. In the same book, he proposes four rules that constitute the right method: the rule of clarity, the rule of analysis, the rule of synthesis, and the rule of completeness (Descartes, 1996, pp. 18–19). First, one must accept as true only what is clearly known. Second, one must divide the subject of investigation into the most basic elements. Third, one must combine these elements into larger units. Fourth, this process should go step by step without jumping.

These rules recur in the pedagogy of Pestalozzi (1995). For him, the method consists of the procedure of analysis, synthesis, and completeness. For language, he asserted that the right method of pedagogy consists of dividing language into its most fundamental elements, such as vowels and consonants, and combining these elements step by step until the meaning of the whole paragraph or book becomes clear. Herbart, whose pedagogy became the official pedagogy of the nineteenth century Germany, inherited this method. It was also imported into Japan in the nineteenth century and remains influential in schools. Today, we still hold that correct teaching and learning should follow such steps.

But what if such a conviction was grossly overrated? It is in this context that the pedagogy of Confucianism and Renaissance humanism merits attention, because they were both prevalent just before the introduction of modern education.

In fact, seen from the perspective of modern pedagogy, both traditions seem to lack a strict form of method.

A book by Battista Guarino (1434–1513), *On the Order of Teaching and Learning* (1459), introduces us the teaching of his father, Guarino da Verona, a famous pedagog of the fifteenth century whose school was visited by pupils from various European countries. When we read this book, we note that despite the title, it contains very little information about methods of teaching and learning, and only scattered remarks about grammar and pronunciation. The central discussion concerns what books to read, instead of how to read them. In the humanistic schools of the Renaissance, pupils learned basic grammar in a short period, and were then required to read the books of classical authors and to memorize many passages.

A similar method (or rather lack of method) is also found in the learning of Confucian texts. In the Edo period, children's learning of Confucian texts was centered on the Four Books. As Tsujimoto remarked, this program started with *sodoku* reading, which consisted of 'reading the scriptures aloud with precision, of repeating it again and again, and of memorizing the whole text completely.' (Tsujimoto, 1999, pp. 52–85) By reading the scriptures with the eyes and reciting them orally, they 'embodied' them (Tsujimoto, 1999, pp. 70–74). Only after having memorized the Four Books completely could students attend their master's lectures and seminars with other students. [This style of learning was shared both by Zhu Xi scholars and Sorai, even though Sorai was unique in recommending reading the text in Chinese rather than using the Japanese version for reading (*kundoku*).]

The first impression we may have of these procedures may be that of amazement and discomfort. It may sound unreasonable to ask pupils to memorize books before teaching them much grammar and vocabulary. And yet, there are also arguments to defend such education.

First, it seems to have functioned well. It succeeded in producing literate men (and some women) versed in classical Latin or classical Chinese. Not only could they read the ancient texts well, but they could also write and speak the ancient languages.

Second, its procedure is in a certain sense more 'natural' in that it corresponds to how we learn our native language. We never learn our native language in the way suggested by Pestalozzi. Instead, we are from the very beginning immersed in the ocean of living language. The whole comes first and the meaning of individual parts comes later.

Third, it cultivates our ears and makes us sensitive to the rhythm and melody of language, which modern education loses by dissecting a language in dead parts.

We should free ourselves from the myth of progress nourished by modern thought and open our ears to other ways of learning that are equally reasonable.

Differences

The comparison between the Confucian and the Western humanistic traditions has so far shown some remarkable similarities. The confirmation of these similarities enlarges our cultural horizon and enables us to envision the liberal, humanistic education of the twenty-first century.

And yet, such confirmation should by no means obfuscate their differences. There are indeed deep differences between the two traditions that should not be overlooked. They concern (1) the medium of language and (2) ritual propriety.

The first difference concerns the priority of written language in the East and spoken language in the West. The investigation of this difference would involve philosophy, history, linguistics, anthropology, and the educational studies. This is a very challenging theme, the investigation of which is beyond the scope of this article.

The second difference concerns the unique role of ritual propriety (*li*) in Confucian tradition.

The translation of this word itself imposes a problem because it has acquired a variety of meanings over the course of history. The impression an average Japanese obtains from this word would either be that of 'manner' in the sense of etiquette, or that of 'discipline.'

The study of Japanese history of education shows that by the Edo period, manners (*saho*) came to be defined as disciplined control of the body. The Ogasawara School of manners is a famous example of this. The manners were incorporated into the Confucian idea of moral education (*shushin*). In 1881, at a time when Japan was zealously introducing Western sciences and discipline into education, the unit of 'manners' was officially admitted as a part of the curriculum for moral education. A strong mixture of Confucianism and Western discipline characterized the education of modern Japan up until 1945. Its influence is still discernible today.

This brief overview suggests a certain continuity between manners and discipline in the East Asian context. The investigation of this theme would bring light to the so-called industriousness of the East Asians.

And yet, we should not forget that the original Confucian concept of *li* had different dimensions: it had its roots in rituals.

According to Kaji, Confucianism that was born after Confucius grew out of 'Proto-Confucianism,' whose essence was shamanism (Kaji, 1990, pp. 52–53). This may account for Confucian scriptures containing so many references to funeral ceremonies. In the 49 chapters of the *Book of Rites*, for example, more than half are dedicated to this theme (Shirakawa, 1991, p. 74). However, this does not mean that Confucius was a shaman. Both Kaji and Shirakawa asserted that Confucius made a distinction between a petty *ru* and a gentleman *ru* (Kaji, 1990, pp. 56–58; Shirakawa, 1991, pp. 72–81). In the *Analects* 6, 13, Confucius says to his disciple Zixia: 'Be a gentleman *ru*, not a petty *ru*' (translation by D. C. Lau (1979) with slight modification). According to Kaji and Shirakawa, a petty *ru* means a shaman in charge of funeral ceremonies, and a gentleman *ru* is an intellectual who is a master *ru*. A gentleman *ru* was not just a performer of rites, but a teacher of rites who understood their theoretical and historical background.

THE CONFUCIAN CONCEPT OF LEARNING

This consideration of the origin of Confucianism enables us to understand the immense importance of ritual propriety for Confucianism. Confucius' predilection for poetry and music should also be placed in this context: they were important because they were necessary elements of rites. This is why Confucius asked his son if he had learned the songs and rites.

This origin of Confucianism stands in clear contrast with the origin of Western humanism.

Western humanism grew out of the ancient rhetoric born in the public space of a Greek polis, especially Athens. Its Roman pioneer, Cicero, was proud to be an active statesman. Salutati and Bruni, humanists of Renaissance Florence, were also actively engaged in politics as secretaries of state. The public space was the focus of Western humanism (Kato, 2014b). This reference to public space makes Western humanistic tradition quite relevant in our age.

When compared to this, Confucianism, with its origin in rituals, might look outdated. And yet, the Confucian *li* with its original connection with rituals can be a useful resource for revisiting our current view of education.

Li is an elaborate system of language and body. Not only our words, but also the entire body must be controlled. When we hear this, we immediately think of discipline or manners. However, two other dimensions should be taken into consideration.

The first is the dimension of communication. When we think of communication, we tend to think almost exclusively of words. And yet, facial expressions, gestures, and tone of voice often play more decisive roles in actual life. These are the modes of communication that we share with animals, and are thus embedded deeply into our organic system.

Confucian *li* is a form of communication. It helps express complex relationships (toward deities, ancestors, parents, etc.) accompanied by appropriate feeling that simple words often fail to express. Simple and straightforward messages are like a picture without a frame. They often mislead and cause offense because they disregard the context in which they occur. Think of e-mail messages, which are especially vulnerable to misunderstanding. This may be the reason why people often use emoticons and other visual signs to indicate their relationship and feeling. An emoticon in this context is a kind of simplified *li*.

The second dimension is that of embodiment of virtues. Sorai develops an interesting argument about this theme.

In the second chapter of *Benmei* named 'Virtue,' Sorai refers to a sentence in the *Book of Rites*: 'Virtue is what a person attains in his body' and criticizes Zhu Xi, who could not free himself from the dualism of heart and body. Thus, Zhu Xi would have considered this passage from the *Book of Rites* to be shallow. But this would only attest to his ignorance of ancient language. In ancient language, 'body (*shen*)' and 'heart (*xin*)' were not antithetical; the word 'body' was understood to encompass the self, including the heart. This is the reason Sorai considered embodiment of virtues as a principal element of learning to be virtuous (Koyasu, 2008, p. 68; Maruyama, 1974, pp. 85–87; Sorai, 2006, p. 182).

Now, this embodiment of virtues is not something each individual does as he or she likes, rather it is deeply rooted in a community (Maruyama, 1974, p. 86). As

Fingarette says, '*Li* is the specifically humanizing form of the dynamic relation of man-to-man.' (Fingarette, 1972, p. 7) And this community, together with virtues, was established by those who first made rites: the early kings (Koyasu, 2008, pp. 71–72). Sorai praised the way of the early kings who governed the heart with rites and criticized those who tried to govern the heart without rites (Koyasu, 2008, p. 95; Sorai, 2006, p. 167). He said: 'Now the early kings realized that language was a relatively insufficient medium with which to instruct (*hua*) people. For that reason, they founded rites and music as a means of teaching them.' (Koyasu, 2008, pp. 132–134; Sorai, 2006, p. 205) According to Sorai, the superiority of rites to words in education lies in their power to transform (*hua*). 'By following the rites, people are transformed.' (Sorai, 2006, p. 205)

These two dimensions of ritual propriety—communication and embodiment—can help us overcome old prejudices predominant in the West. They concern the priority of (human) language to other forms of communication and the priority of consciousness (or mind) to body. The first prejudice has its roots in ancient Greece. The second prejudice also originated from Greek experience, but became especially prevalent in Europe after the seventeenth century. Both prejudices are also related, in that they stand in opposition to what belongs to the body. Both stress the difference between man and animal, mind and body, and reason and desire. The education, accordingly, is conceived as a transition from the latter to the former, or as the control of the latter by the former. Even the education of manners developed in modern Europe was fed by this mistrust of the body (Elias, 1994). The strong antipathy to body fluids may be a reflection of this (Taylor, 2007, pp. 136–142). A similar fear of the body is also characteristic of Western discipline. As Foucault demonstrated, the repression of the sexual was one of the driving forces of Western discipline (Foucault, 1976).

The danger of these prejudices is that they easily overlook that articulated human language and consciousness are only a tip of the iceberg of what it means to be human. Such neglect of the physical body can often produce pathological disturbances not only in individuals, but also in society and the environmental sphere, as Gregory Bateson repeatedly warned (Bateson, 2000).

It is therefore advisable for the theory of education to evaluate and make positive use of our bodily existence. The role of ritual propriety in Confucian learning can be instructive in this sense. Of course, this does not mean that we introduce rites into schools. Placed in the context of modern education, such rites would easily become a yet another form of discipline. And yet, education can help to broaden our understanding of communication so that we can appreciate and become sensitive to the full dimensions of non-verbal interaction, which range from simple gestures to various forms of arts. Education should also take embodied learning into more consideration. Here, the East Asian tradition of the way of skill (*geido*) may be instructive. Such consideration may help us to appreciate the educational power of arts and sport.

In summary, the Confucian humanistic tradition not only corroborates the humanistic education of the West, but can modify its course in a direction that is less 'anthropocentric' and therefore more humane and human.

Disclosure statement

No potential conflict of interest was reported by the author.

References

Ames, R. T., & Rosemont Jr., H. (1998). *The analects of Confucius*. New York, NY: The Random House Publishing Group.
Bateson, G. (2000). *Steps to an ecology of mind*. Chicago, IL: The University of Chicago Press.
Chang, W. (1969). *A sourcebook in Chinese philosophy*. Princeton, NJ: Princeton University Press.
Descartes, R. (1996). Discours de la Méthode [Discourse on the Method]. In publiées par Ch. Adam et P. Tannery, *Oevres de Descartes* [Works of Descartes] (Vol. 6, pp. 1–78). Paris: Vrin.
Elias, N. (1994). *The civilizing process*, revised edition (E. Jephcott, Trans.). London: Blackwell.
Fingarette, H. (1972). *Confucius: The secular as sacred*. Long Grove, IL: Waveland Press.
Foucault, M. (1976). *Histoire de la sexualité: La volonté de savoir* [The history of sexuality. The will to knowledge]. Paris: Gallimard.
Gadamer, H.-G. (1975). *Wahrheit und Methode* [Truth and method]. Tuebingen: J. C. B. Mohr.
Garin, E. (1975). *Educazione umanistica in Italia* [Humanistic education in Italy]. Bari: Laterza.
Grendler, P. F. (1989). *Schooling in renaissance Italy: Literacy and learning 1300–1600*. Baltimore, MD: The John Hopkins University Press.
Kaji, N. (1990). *Jukyo toha nanika* [What is confucianism?]. Tokyo: Chuko Shinsho.
Kato, M. (1992). Leonardo Bruni to Cicero-Kyoyoron wo megutte [Leonardo Bruni and Cicero. Concerning the theory of culture]. *Studi Italici, 42*, 56–79.
Kato, M. (2014a). Humanistic education in East Asia. *Zeitschrift fuer Paedagogik, 60*, 96–108.
Kato, M. (2014b). Significance of the rhetorical and humanistic tradition for education today. *Asia Pacific Education Review, 15*, 55–63.
Kimball, B. A. (1986). *Orators and philosophers: A history of the idea of liberal education*. New York, NY: Teachers College Press.
Kondo, T. (1984). *Petoraruka Kenkyu* [Studies on Petrarch]. Tokyo: Sobunsha.
Koyasu, N. (2008). *Sorai-gaku Kogi: Benmei wo yomu* [Lectures on Sorai's Benmei]. Tokyo: Iwanami Shoten.
Kristeller, P. O. (1955). *The classics and renaissance thought*. Cambridge, MA: Harvard University Press.
Lau, D. C. (1979). *Confucius, the Analects*. London: Penguin Books.
Leeman, A., & Pinkster, H. (1981). *M. Tullius Cicero: De oratore libri III* [M. Tullius Cicero, De orator, three volumes], 1. Band. Heidelberg: Carl Winter.
Lidin, O. G. (1973). *The life of Ogyu Sorai, a Tokugawa Confucian Philosopher*. Lund: Scandinavian Institute of Asian Studies (Monograph Series No. 19).
Marrou, H. I. (1981). *Histoire de l'éducation dans l'Antiquité* [The history of education in antiquity]. Paris: Seuil.
Maruyama, M. (1974). *Studies in intellectual history in Tokugawa Japan*. (M. Hane, Trans.). Tokyo: University of Tokyo Press.
Morohashi, T. (1973). *Rongo no kenkyu* [Studies on the analects]. Tokyo: Daishukan Shoten.

Pestalozzi, J. (1995). *Wie Gertrud ihre Kinder lehrt* [How Gertrude taught her children]. Reprint of 1801 edition. Bristol: Thoemmes Press.
Shirakawa, S. (1991). *Koushi Den* [The life of Confucius]. Tokyo: Chuko Bunko.
Sorai, O. (2006). *Ogyu Sorai's philosophical masterworks*. Honolulu: Association for Asian Studies and University of Hawaii Press.
Taylor, C. (2007). *A secular age*. Cambridge, MA: Belknap Press.
Tsujimoto, M. (1999). *Manabi no fukken: mohou to shujuku* [Restoration of learning: Imitation and practice]. Tokyo: Kadokawa Shoten.
Tu, W. (1993). *Way, learning, and politics: Essays on the Confucian intellectual*. Albany: State University of New York Press.
Voigt, G. (1960). *Die Wiederbelebung des klassischen Altertums, vierte unveraenderte Auflage* [The revival of classical antiquity, the fourth edition]. Berlin: Walter de Gruyter.
Yoshikawa, K. (1975). *Jinsai, Sorai, Norinaga*. Tokyo: Iwanami Shoten.

"The Source of Learning is Thought" Reading the *Chin-ssu lu* (近思錄) with a "Western Eye"

ROLAND REICHENBACH

Abstract

The contribution focuses on Neo-Confucian texts as collected by Zhu Xi (朱熹 1130–1200) and Lü Zuqian (1137–1181) and is a look from the 'outside', from the perspective of German theories of Bildung ('self-cultivation'). It aims at demonstrating that among other insights that today's readers may gather from Neo-Confucian literature, one aspect protrudes from others: that learning can be considered as a virtue—even a meta-virtue—a form of life and mode of self-formation of the person. It does not seem exaggerated, from this perspective, to state that Neo-Confucian philosophy is—to a large extent—a philosophy of learning and self-transformation which offers fruitful irritants for questioning the widespread habits of thinking about skills and their development in today's strong and problematic discourses and corresponding educational policies.

> Without learning there will be no means
> of entering Tao. The efforts in becoming a sage
> or a worthy lie completely in learning.
> After knowing the road to follow,
> and getting in the right direction to advance,
> we can speak about learning
> (Chu Hsi, 1991, p. 73).

Preliminary Remarks

Among the various insights that today's readers may gather from Confucian (and especially Neo-Confucian) literature, one aspect seems to protrude from others: that learning can be considered as a virtue—even a *meta*-virtue—a form of life and mode of self-formation of the person. It does not seem exaggerated to state that Neo-Confucian philosophy is—to a large extent—a philosophy of learning and self-transformation which offers a great opportunity for critical reflections on today's rather superficial and instrumentalist understanding of learning.

The influence of Confucian thinking and pertinent concepts has been marginal in the German history of educational thought. This somewhat contrasts with its impact on German philosophy, whose exponents—on not so rare occasions, at least—have referred to the work and life of Confucius. Confucius, according to German philosopher Karl Jaspers, is one of the four most influential human beings in the world history of thought (cf. Jaspers, 1964). But in contrast to the other three 'big names'—Socrates, Buddha, and Jesus—Confucius left written works to posterity. Unfortunately perhaps, they have not yet been authenticated. Nevertheless, being aware of the importance of and focus on learning and the idea of self-transformation in Confucian thinking, it remains more than just surprising that reference to the Chinese tradition has been rather spare in German thinking (as well as in other European language cultures and educational discourses). Even worse, the superficial image of Confucius is that of a moralizing father figure whose anecdotes and locutions are collected in little phrase books suitable as gifts for special social occasions but probably not taken seriously in the academic context—outside the Sinology departments, of course. The public reception of Confucius—in contrast to Jesus, Buddha, and Socrates—may even show some clownish streaks. Therefore, the importance of Confucian institutes all over the world seems obvious.

In the following pages, I will have a look at Neo-Confucian texts as collected by Zhu Xi (1130–1200) and Lü Zuqian (1137–1181).[1] It is a modest look from the 'outside', from the perspective of German theories of *Bildung* ('self-cultivation'). It is interesting, on one the hand, to focus on parallels of humanistic concepts of learning and education while examining the much older thoughts and insights as presented in the Neo-Confucian texts named above on the other. A crucial difficulty in both cases is the problem of differentiating between normative and descriptive aspects or statements in Neo-Confucian notions as well as in humanistic concepts of learning and self-transformation. I will focus on (what I would like to call) the *ethos* of learning rather than the role and importance of morality in Confucian thinking (cf. Ivanhoe, 1993) and Zhu Xi's moral psychology (cf. Shun, 2010). This may occur due to a (personal) lack of insight, but, by reading the *Chin-ssu lu,* one might develop the impression that it is not implausible to reconstruct Neo-Confucian perspectives on learning (in some respects, at least) by noting the concepts of negativity and negative morality which border on the 'aporetic' style of Socratic thinking (as presented in the earlier phase of Plato's work). And it remains striking that Confucius and Socrates lived at about the same period of time (Socrates 469–399 BC, Confucius 551–479 BC). However, I am unfortunately not in a position to fulfill this interesting task. Rather I will focus on the idea of '*learning by thinking*' which demands epistemic virtues—most of all modesty in evaluating one's own knowledge, which is an ethos of learning.

With such a concept ('ethos'), the problem of the entangling cognitive and ethical aspects cannot be resolved; I am aware of this, and I know that this is less than what a 'pure analytical' view can accept. Nevertheless, the possible 'accusation' (or misinterpretation)—according to which Neo-Confucian thoughts on learning are mainly ways to moralize the topic—can be rejected.

Yet the study of Neo-Confucian texts on learning seems to offer fruitful irritants for questioning the widespread habits of thinking about skills and their development in today's strong and problematic discourses and corresponding educational policies.

The Chin-ssu lu

The *Chin-ssu lu* is a collection of Neo-Confucian thoughts on metaphysics, ethics, reading and literature, and government. It also reflects on Chinese history and its heterodox systems, Buddhism and Taoism. Wing-Tsit Chan calls the *Chin-ssu lu* 'Neo-Confucianism in a nutshell' and explains: 'Since it is the forerunner and model of the Hsing-li ta-ch'üan [*Great collection of Neo-Confucianism*] which was the standard text covering Chinese thoughts for 500 years, its tremendous influence on Chinese philosophy can easily be imagined' (Chin-ssu lu, 1967, ix). Whereas Wang Yang-ming's *Instructions on the Practical Living* represents the major work of the *idealistic* wing of Neo-Confucianism, according to Wing-Tsit Chan, the *Chin-ssu lu* is the major work of the *rationalistic* wing of Neo-Confucianism. 'It is no exaggeration to say (...)', he continues, 'that it has been the most important book in China for the last 750 years' (ix). Only a fraction of the Neo-Confucian works had been translated into Western languages up to the 1960's. The translation of the *Chin-ssu lu* (to Wing-Tsit Chan, at least) was 'imperative' and 'long overdue'. The 1967 translation includes many comments by Chinese, Korean, and Japanese scholars. Another reader on (and of) Zhu Xi, 'Further Reflections on Things at Hand', was published in 1991.

The *Chin-ssu lu* was written and compiled in 1175 during the Song dynasty (960–1279), almost 17 centuries after the *Lunyu*. De Bary writes in '*Principle and Practicality: Essay in Neo-Confucianism and Practical Learning*' (edited in 1979 by Theodore de Bary and Irene Bloom) about the Song dynasty:

> Despite their access to power and the benevolent patronage of Song rulers, the Song Confucians had encountered human limitations in the executing of their grand designs. (...) Chu Hsi (Zhu Xi), in the twelfth century, readjusted and reordered his human priorities. The consequence was his intensification of the effort to articulate Neo-Confucian metaphysics and to develop a practical system of spiritual and intellectual cultivation, centering on the ideal of the sage .... (De Bary, 1979, p. 10)

In this process, Neo-Confucianism developed features with strong resemblances to later European Renaissance and its central topics such as

> the dignity of man, the immortality of the soul, and the unity of truth. Each of these has a close counterpart in the central doctrines of Neo-Confucianism. Though the second theme is expressed in terms quite different from Confucianism, e.g. immortality of the soul, the Neo-Confucians had a religious or mystical view of the self as united with all creation in such a way as to transcend its finite limitations. This is found most characteristically in Neo-Confucian accounts of attaining sage-hood as an experience of

realizing the true self, based on the doctrine that 'humaneness unites man with Heaven-and-Earth and all things'. (De Bary, 1979, p. 10–11)

In the Chinese case, de Bary explains, on the one hand, the

> reaffirmation of humane values took on a special quality as a reaction against Buddhism; on the other, certain characteristic features of Neo-Confucianism showed the influence of Buddhism. The net result, then, was a humanistic revival which did not so much result in a decline of spirituality as in a transformation of it. (p. 7)

Be it this or another way, it may seem appropriate to say that this resembles the Renaissance return to a classical heritage in the eleventh-century revival and restoration of Confucianism.

East–West comparisons: A Note on Simplistic Dichotomies, and the Request to Doubt

Also Western non-experts in Confucianism, non-sinologists, and people fully ignorant of Chinese history and language, may today feel quite comfortable in the lecture on the *Chin-ssu lu*, the more *rationalistic* wing of Neo-Confucianism, which offers striking resemblances to some aspects of the *Bildung* idea. The German notion of *Bildung* is usually traced back to Eckhart von Hochheim (known as 'Meister Eckhart'), who lived from 1260 to 1328 and was quite an influential theologian and philosopher of the late Middle Age. The concept of *Bildung* is of *theological* and *spiritual* origins, not mainly a concept of Enlightenment rationality, as it is sometimes interpreted in a rather reductionist manner.

Whenever it comes to the notion of the *self* and the notion of *rationality*, some authors feel quite tempted to make rather dualistic and simple statements or comparisons between Eastern and Western thoughts. This may be to keep things simple. But it may be politically motivated or derived from pure ignorance, or reflect a desire to establish certainties in matters of cultural identity and heritage. Whatever the source or motives may be, such dualistic propositions are not convincing, while being historically ranked as philosophically untenable. Unfortunately, one comes across many such simplistic East–West dualisms and dichotomies.[2] It's a wonder how the authors could develop such 'great' overviews and feel so certain that they were capable of comparing *the* Confucian tradition with *the* Western tradition. Doubt, of course, was not invented by René Descartes. As we know, it had already played a major role in the Socratic tradition. One may read in the *Chin-ssu lu*: 'The student must first of all know how to doubt' (Chin-ssu lu, III, 15, [1967, p. 94]). Neither the Socratic nor the Confucian tradition is a homogenous body of thought, insights, inspirations, and questions. Those who enter such a tradition gain a contact with an entire *universe*, not just a simple body of anecdotes and phrases. You do not compare universes! If one could compare universes, one might dispense with doubts and questions. Even worse, one would not have started to study the universe at all:

> People who do not doubt simply have not been devoted to concrete practice. If they have concretely practiced, there must be some doubts. Something must be impracticable, and that raises questions. (Chin-ssu lu, II, 102, [1967, p. 85])

Commenting on the Confucian tradition, one should be more or less familiar with 18 dynasties and their spiritual, religious, and political circumstances. Comments on Western thinking may also require pertinent insights into the history of thoughts from antiquity to postmodern times. But, of course, our lives are too short for such endeavors. We can only comfort ourselves with fragmented insights and get in touch with the universe of the unknowns. Yet our ambitions should not be too modest:

> It is very important that a student should not have a small ambition or to be flippant. If his ambition is small, he will be easily satisfied. If he is easily satisfied, there will be no way for him to advance. Being flippant, he will think that he already knows what he does not yet know and that he has studied what he has not yet studied. (Chin-ssu lu, II, 111, [1967, p. 87])

In quoting this passage, of course, I implicitly refer not only to Confucius but also to Socrates. To become educated means to learn what one does not know.

> We must try to know what we do not yet know, and to correct what is not good in us, however little. This is the improvement of our moral nature. (Chin-ssu lu, II, 94, [1967, p. 83])

Knowing about what one does *not* know is neither a sign of ignorance nor indifference but rather the starting point of learning. To make not-knowing explicit is an expression of thinking and insight. This major feature of a so-called negative pedagogy can already be found in the *Analects* (Lunyu) as well as in the Platonic reference to the aporetic side of Socrates. It remains striking how during the same era (in Greek antiquity and the Chunqiu dynasty) the figures of Socrates and Confucius articulate agnostic and negative wisdom—among other similarities (and, of course, important differences, see, e.g. Tweed & Lehman, 2002).

The Ethos and Love of Learning

A wonderful and well-known passage in *the Analects* concerns critical students. 'The Master said, Yan Hui was not any help to me, for he always accepted everything I said' (Lun yü, XI, 4, Confucius, 1979, p. 106). According to Paul (2006, 2010), Confucius expresses here that learning becomes more difficult if the learner fails to contradict or offer criticism—at least from time to time (Paul, 2010, p. 46). Learning is about thinking. You may be intelligent but not focus on thinking. On the other hand, you may be not so bright but familiar with the practice of thinking and studying.[3] That is important for self-cultivation, because 'the source of learning is thought' (Chin-ssu lu, III, 6, [1967, p. 90]).

The close connection between learning and thinking requires an effort to look for expressions that fit personal experiences:

> Whenever in our effort at thinking we come to something that cannot be expressed in words, we must think it over carefully and sift it clearly again and again. Only this can be considered skillful learning. As for Kao Tzu, whenever he came to something that could not be expressed in words, he would stop and inquire no more. (Chin-ssu lu, III, 22, [1967, p. 97])

Learning, for many students, is naturally no fun at all, and most students want to avoid the effort to think and learn or agree to learn only if it is smooth and easy. This is not a new phenomenon:

> Nowadays students study like people climbing a hill. As long as the path is unobstructed and leveled, they take long steps. When they reach a dangerous point, they stop right away. The thing to do is to be firm and determined and proceed with resolution and courage. (Chin-ssu lu, II, 53, [1967, p. 62])

There is no doubt that students—in this traditional view—can be clearly separated into at least two groups: students who possess the capacity to struggle and push themselves forward, and those who lack this disposition and virtue. 'Now as for persons with inferior capacity who wish to pursue learning at leisure and allow it to proceed wherever it pleases—I have never heard that such a person can succeed' (Chin-ssu lu, II, 92, [1967, p. 82]).

It is important to understand that the major motive for learning and thinking in the Confucian view is a special kind of *fondness* or *love*. 'If someone engages in idle speculation at home, and neither studies nor inquires, then he is already a normal commoner. That which gives a sage his sageliness is fondness for learning and inquiry from inferiors' (Chu Hsi 1991, p. 73). Learning, and the love of learning, can therefore be regarded as a sort of *meta-virtue* which forms the base and precondition of self-cultivation. This grand view is already expressed by Confucius himself:

> To love benevolence *ren*(仁) without loving learning is liable to lead to foolishness. To love cleverness without loving learning is liable to lead to deviation from the right path. To love trustworthiness in word without loving learning is liable to lead to harmful behavior. To love forthrightness without loving learning is liable to lead to intolerance. To love courage without loving learning is liable to lead to insubordination. To love unbending strength without loving learning is liable to lead to indiscipline. (Confucius, 1979, XVII, 8, pp. 144–145)

Personal dignity, self-respect, and social recognition—in this view—depend less on achieved skills than on effort (virtues) to change. The language of virtues is richer, for it includes people's willingness, desire, and motivation, not just as a necessary drive to acquire skills or act accordingly but as an inherent feature of human practice.

The ethos of learning is not just a willingness to push oneself forward in an obsessive way to gather knowledge and skills.

> People say we must practice with effort. Such a statement, however, is superficial. If a person really knows what a thing should be done, he does

not need to wait for his will to be aroused. As soon as he artificially arouses will, that means selfishness. How can such a spirit last long? (Chin-ssu lu, II, 54, [1967, p. 63])

'Do what you must' serves as the maxim and ethos of learning; it stresses being ambitious without absolutely wanting to reach the target. Therefore, one could seek the 'pleasure of learning' or learning as a form of living.

One who knows learning will surely love it. He who loves it will surely seek it. And he who seeks it will surely achieve it. The learning of the ancients is a lifetime affair. If in moments of haste and in times of difficulty or confusion one is devoted to it, how can one fail to achieve it? (Chin-ssu lu, II, 55, [1967, p. 63])

What was said in the section above may remind one—to some degree—of John Dewey's a-teleological theory of learning and education, the idea of learning without focusing on a target outside the process of learning. 'Master Ming-Tao said: In learning we must avoid setting up a target. If we go step by step without stop, we will succeed' (Chin-ssu lu, II, 74, [1967, p. 69]). In the further notes: Someone asked, 'In his endeavor, a student should aim at becoming a sage. Why not set up a target?' Zhu Xi answered:

Of course a student should regard a sage as his teacher, but what need is there to set up a target? As soon as one sets up a target, his mind will be calculating and deliberating as when he will become a sage and what the stage of sagehood will be like. Thus from the start in his mind he puts success ahead of effort. (...) If every day we compare ourselves with others this way or that way, it will not do. (...) If one first sets up a target, he will surely get into the trouble of aiming too high or trying short cuts. (p. 70)

'In learning', Zhu Xi says in the *Further Reflections on Things at Hand*, 'do not reach for the clouds or overextend yourself. Simply examine words and deeds, and there is your reality' (Chu Hsi 1991, S.74). Ambition and uptightness seem to be regarded as the enemies of true learning. The intention or even obsession to attain the goal of sagacity seems to be the perfect way to miss the (implicit) goal.

In the pursuit of learning, if one's intention is first of all toward accomplishment, he will hurt his learning. With that intention, he will try to bore through things in violation of principle and to make up things, thus leading to a lot of trouble. (Chin-ssu lu, II, 106, [1967, p. 85])

And:

The student must devote himself to reality. He should not be attracted to fame. If he has any desire for fame, he is insincere. The great foundation is already lost. What is there to be learned? Although devotion to fame and devotion to profit differ in the degree of impurity, their selfish motivation is the same. (Chin-ssu lu, II, 62, [1967, p. 67])

One must move on step by step. This pedagogical insight is so important to Zhu Xi that his work is called 'Chin-ssu lu', meaning something like 'reflections on things at hand': 'Question: What is meant by reflection on things at hand? Answer: To extend the basis of similarity in kind' (Chin-ssu lu, III, 14, [1967, p. 94]).

There is a multifaceted history to tell about developing the canonized work in Confucian thinking and about its transformations—'de-canonizations' and 're-canonizations'. The shift veers away from the *Five Classics*[4] to the *Four Books* in the Song period, a shift which represents a move toward inwardness (cf. Gardener, 2007, p. xxii). Zhu Xi (Zhu Xi) as earlier Song literati was mainly interested and attracted to the *Analects*, the *Mencius*, the *Great Learning*, and *Maintaining Perfect Balance* (p. xxiii). A 'number of the greatest Confucian literati of the Song not only counted Buddhists among their close acquaintances but themselves had studied Buddhist teachings' (...) 'They were poised for the shift inward' (ibid.). It is a shift from topics of community and governance to more general matters of human nature. Could one call it an anthropological turn?[5]

Interruption: The Turn to Inwardness (East and West ...)

Zhou Dunyi (1017–1073) promoted Yan Hui as the true student of Confucius (Hon, 2010, p. 13). By doing this, Zhou 'redefined learning as an individual quest for cultivating the mind', argued Hon (2010). This turn is also found in ancient Greek philosophy, especially Platonic thinking (Platon, 1993, 1996) and the concept of 'care for the self' (Foucault, 1993; Hadot, 1981, 1996), and in neo-humanistic philosophy (Humboldt, 1969). Both the Confucian and the Platonic turns to inwardness started from a political context, the context of human action. As Hon explains:

> A learned person, then, is not just a person of action. He is also a person of the right mind who recognizes the inherent connections among all beings in this universe. This 'inward turning is to make cultivation of the heart/mind the most important part of human learning. (Hon, 2010, p. 13)

This ideal is also found in the humanistic notion of self-cultivation and self-transformation, for which Wilhelm von Humboldt used the (originally pietistic and theological) term *Bildung* (Koller, 1999; Kühne, 1976). It is therefore *not* a German specialty or exclusivity, of course (as is sometimes stated in the educational and cultural discourse, especially in Germany [see e.g. Bollenbeck, 1996]). However, one might not exaggerate to state that the ideal of *self-cultivation* is a most elaborated and sophisticated Confucian and Neo-Confucian thought (Wei-ming, 1979), whereas the concept of the *self* is much articulated and differentiated in humanistic tradition (Taylor, 1989).

The German concept of *Bildung* 'refers to the inner development of the individual, a process of fulfillment through education and knowledge, in effect a secular search for perfection, representing progress and refinement in both knowledge and moral terms, an amalgam of wisdom and self-realization' (Watson, 2010, pp. 53–54). It may be important to consider that the German Enlightenment (*Aufklärung*) came later in history than the French, English, and Scottish Enlightenment. The German *Aufklärer*

—'men of Enlightenment'—could borrow from their neighbors and their earlier achievements, and they 'did so selectively, to address problems of specific concern in German intellectual life' (Watson, 2010, p. 69).

Enlightenment thought, in general, was characterized by the rise of historicism. Whereas the idea of societal change was widely accepted in late-seventeenth century and early eighteenth century Europe, the German Enlightenment focused specifically on the direction, logic, and meaningfulness of change. Initially, German intellectuals were fascinated by the French Revolution, though later disgusted by the post-revolutionary terror. This was a remarkable backlash to their hope for political progress. Without oversimplifying things, one may state that the main difference between the French and German Enlightenment is a differing understanding of freedom due to the varying historic experiences before and after the French revolution. Whereas in the early Western Enlightenment period freedom was understood as an outward, definitely political concept, in the later German Enlightenment the predominant understanding of freedom was characterized by rather an esthetic dimension: not outward but internal freedom. Even the concept of the so-called *Bildungsstaat* ('state/nation of *Bildung*') as proposed by historicist *Aufklärer*, was mainly an esthetic idea—'a state whose main ideal was to enrich the inner life of man' (Watson, 2010, p. 77). For Wilhelm von Humboldt, *Bildung* as 'education through the humanities' was 'the true path to inner freedom' (p. 832).

The shift from a political understanding of Enlightenment—like in France, England, and Scotland—to German *inwardness* ('*Innerlichkeit*'), as realized by the concept of *Bildung*, can be interpreted—at least to a certain degree—as a desire of German intellectuals to escape from a brutal and on the whole disappointing post-revolutionary world to a place where man could seek secular perfection: an escape toward inwardness. Therefore, the German concept of humanist *Bildung* can be criticized as an apolitical ideal in a discourse environment where questions and topics of political rights, social justice, and societal change were increasingly neglected. That might be one reason why in history humanist *Bildung* became entangled later in Germany with political conservatism and social snobbery (Watson, 2010, p. 834).[6]

The Effort and Imposition of Studying

The study of the *Four Books* for boys and young men was surely 'arduous and not necessarily intellectually challenging or stimulating'. Most of the time was probably spent in rote memorization (Gardener, 2007, p. xiii). This was surely necessary in order to succeed in the first stage of civil service examinations, at the district level, and to move on to an examination in the provincial capital, and then, after success there, being qualified to participate at a set of examinations in the imperial capital. The Four Books 'were considered sacred texts, for they were the direct words and teachings of the great sages of antiquity, men whose exemplary wisdom and virtues served as an eternal model for the ages' (Gardener, 2007, p. xv). Therefore, one must consider the significance of these books as of the Bible in the West, its 'passages, lines, and terms (…) became part of the *lingua franca* in China' (ibid.).

THE CONFUCIAN CONCEPT OF LEARNING

Even though examination candidates were expected for hundreds of years (at least from 1300 to 1900) to demonstrate their mastery of the *Four Books*—the *Great Learning*, the *Analects*, the *Mencius*, and *Maintaining Perfect Balance*, as well as Zhu Xi's comments on them, we must think of their performances as the results of hard rote-learning efforts.

Of course, one will find many passages in the *Chin-ssu lu* which suggest that memorization is maybe necessary but not enough. At the center of educational progress and perfection lies pre-occupation with the not yet known:

> We must try to know what we do not yet know, and to correct what is not good in us, however little. This is the improvement of our moral nature. In studying books, search for moral principles. In compiling books, appreciate what ultimate purposes they have. Do not just copy them. In addition, know much about words and deeds of former sages and worthies. This is the improvement of our inquiry and study. Do not relax for a moment. Keep on like this for three years, and there will be progress. (Chin-ssu lu, II, 94, [1967, p. 83])

There have been curricular debates, and the specialist can reconstruct rather precisely which contents were regarded as valuable, improper, or even dangerous during the very many periods of Confucian thinking:

> The learning of the ancients consisted of only one thing, whereas the learning of today consists of three things, not including the heterodoxial doctrines [meaning Buddhism and Taoism]. The first is literacy composition; the second, textual criticism; and the third, Confucianism. If one wishes to advance toward the Way, nothing other than Confucianism will do. (Chin-ssu lu, II, 56, [1967, p. 63])

To a large extent, the passages on learning in the *Chin-ssu lu* are about the right attitude of successful learning, the ethos of learning which includes the learner's confidence, equability, persistence, and, most of all, modesty. The latter can be experienced in the willingness to learn from people with socially inferior status.

> Many people think they are mature and experienced and therefore are not willing to learn from their inferiors. Consequently they remain ignorant all their lives. Some people regard themselves as the first ones to know moral principles and for them there is no such thing as ignorance. Consequently they too are not willing to learn from inferiors. Because they are never willing to learn, they think of many things that deceive themselves and others. They are willing to remain ignorant throughout their lives. (Chin-ssu lu, II, 98, [1967, p. 94])

Thinking of oneself as being mature and experienced will be an obstacle for learning and therefore for moving on in personal development. Even though the ethos of learning is about moving on step by step, about not being too eager or ambitious, the proper learner learns *as if* he or she would want to become a sage.

THE CONFUCIAN CONCEPT OF LEARNING

> Only when people have the will to seek to become sages can we study together with them. Only when they can study and think carefully can we proceed with them toward the Way. Only when they can think with success can we get established in the Way together with them. When they are thoroughly transformed with it, we can then weigh events with them, as to which is standard and which is expedient. (Chin-ssu lu, II, 65, [1967, p. 67])

The obstacles in moving on, the difficulties in life, are the essential materials for the possibility of self-transformation. *The Chin-ssu lu* can be regarded as a very early if not the earliest document to understand the importance of *discontinuity* in learning and the role of discontinuity for personal development.[7]

> Difficulties improve a person because they help him discriminate moral values carefully and they make his sensitivity greater. This is why Mencius said, 'Men who have the wisdom of virtues and the knowledge of skill are always found to have experienced great difficulties. (Chin-ssu lu, II, 87, [1967, p. 76])

Great difficulties, also smaller difficulties, of course, put a person in a 'disequilibrium' (Piaget, 1957), at least in some 'cognitive dissonance' (Festinger, 1957); it is striking how differentiated the insights into these problems and their potential for personal development are expressed in *the Chin-ssu lu*. Willingness and effort to find equilibrium requires an antecedent state of problem or disequilibrium, of uncertainty and of a need for a change.

> Before one makes up his mind, the trouble is that he has too many ideas and is uncertain. After he has made up his mind, the trouble is that his study and cultivation are not refined. Thoughts of study and of cultivation are all matters of learning. Pursue it diligently. Why get tired of it? One must lose no time in seeking what is desirable in order to get his mind established in a position of certainty. Then he can go ahead easily like a river bursting forth. (Chin-ssu lu, II, 92, [1967, p. 82])

However, the most striking insights Western readers can take from the lecture of the Chin-ssu lu—at least to me—is something which seems so fundamental and obvious that it has been underestimated and indeed almost forgotten in today's pedagogical and didactical theories: learning is a social matter, not purely individual. The learner needs another person who shows him something, be it intended or not. The cultivation of the self is a social matter. Here, it seems, that the Socratic or Platonic idea of *care for the self* and the Confucian ideal of self-cultivation seem to share a common ground; let me say, an amazingly common ground:

> In one's words there should be something to teach others. In one's activities there should be something to serve as a model for others. In the morning something should be done. In the evening something should be realized. At every moment something should be nourished. And in every instant something should be preserved. (Chin-ssu lu, II, 88, [1967, p. 76])

THE CONFUCIAN CONCEPT OF LEARNING

Closing Remarks: Reading the Chin-ssu lu with a 'Western Eye'

Some familiarity with the discourse of *Bildung* offers opportunities to detect and recognize crucial questions and ideas on the importance of learning in the cultivation of the self as presented in the *Chin-ssu lu*. During the course of the past two centuries, there has been a considerable change in the concept of Bildung within the connotational field (Hörster, 1995). Yet the genealogical origins of the concept mentioned above are in medieval mysticism and pietistic theology. Whereas *Bildung* in the eighteenth century was closely connected with the idea of 'humanity' and 'perfection' (concepts such as Enlightenment, bringing virtue and spirit together by the idea of *Bildung*), at the end of the nineteenth century Bildung became understood as a commodity and a value. Since the mid-twentieth century, during the course of establishing the social sciences in the broad educational discourse, there have been attempts to replace the concept of *Bildung* by concepts such as deculturation, socialization, ego-identity, development, and qualification. Thus, the concept of Bildung also experienced periods of trivialization and sometimes complete transformation.

The ambiguity and vulnerability of the (original) concept of *Bildung* have nevertheless not resulted in the idea of *Bildung* having satisfyingly been replaced by surrogates as suggested by different sides (Pleines, 1989, p. 1). Pleines (1971) suggested that an attempt to systematize the educational meaning of the *Bildung* concept is still convincing today. He knows fully well that a 'premature determination of its meaning or a structural reduction of its original meaning will result in its decline and thus in the leveling of its originally intended contents' (p. 12). Pleines refers to (1) '*Bildung* as a valuable commodity which must be strived for', (2) '*Bildung* as a state of mind', (3) '*Bildung* as a process of mind', (4) '*Bildung* as a permanent task', (5) '*Bildung* as man's self-fulfillment in freedom', and finally pointing out to (6) 'educated (*gebildet*) man and his/her *Bildung* of reason and heart' (see pp. 12–38).

The reader of the *Chin-ssu lu* will detect all these aspects (or comparable ideas, at least) in this grand collection of texts. The cultivated individual, the learner striving for self-cultivation, is—in the Confucian tradition—considered as a unity. It might easily be overseen that the idea of *Bildung* is not an analytical notion (at least in its origins), but rather—and similar to the (Neo-) Confucian idea of self-cultivation—Bildung is originally regarded as *mediator* between the 'unity of the individual' and the 'totality of the world' (Posner, 1988, p. 26). This mediation is either viewed as a process, a state (or goal), or both. The ideals of educational objectives even in today's discourses (such as responsibility, independence, self-determination, reasonable practice, etc.) thus provide the concept of *Bildung* with its 'typical dignity' and make it a regulative idea of general education and educational theory with 'a place of normative understanding within it' (Miller-Kipp, 1992, pp. 18–19). The constitutive core of the *Bildung* idea seems so close to the Confucian ideal of the person learning to care for oneself on his or her own. In whichever way the term of *Bildung* is used (as a critical term for judging practical work or as an 'uncritical' term which can be ideologized and used), what remains as the actual point of reference of the *Bildung* concept is the subject as a *self-educating individual* or an individual under education. Hence, the 'idea of the subject' becomes the 'systematic core of the concept of *Bildung*, and the question of the subject in the process of *Bildung* is the fundamental question of *Bildung*' (ibid. p. 19). Thus, educational theory cannot avoid questions concerning the subject's constitution—not only in the philosophical sense but also in the psychological and sociological one.

Despite the 'blurred' definition of *Bildung*, as a 'universal topic'—if we knew what that is, after all—*Bildung* (at least in the German-speaking world)—will stay 'up to date' as long as humans are supposed to be supported and assisted on their way toward some version of the ideal of self-formation. This also implies certain anthropologic presumptions. The ontological and normative definitions of understanding oneself and the world will be up to date as long as people consider themselves as 'self-interpreting animals' (Taylor, 1985) or self-interpreting creatures (Fink, 1970, p. 193). Any concept of *Bildung*—or self-cultivation—necessarily transports or reflects the world views of and images of man. Educational concepts have always been and are still influenced by the predominant political and cultural situation, which may result in rather a euphoric and/or elitist educational discourse. For instance, identifying *Bildung* with a narrow concept of culture, as was common among the German bourgeoisie in the nineteenth century, understanding it as being different from everyday matters and civilization, resulted in perceiving a huge gap between '*Gebildeten*' (educated people) and '*Ungebildeten*' (uneducated people) or '*Volk*' (the lower classes) (Hörster, 1995, pp. 46f).

In mass societies, actually just a few individuals can become educated i.e. according to the ideals of Greek antiquity. It may be that educational capital understood in this sense will not have any 'equalizing' effect on given social structures if 'equalization' is its essential topic. Despite any individual acquisition of education, the unequal distribution of educational capital or unequal access to education will result in an analogous division along with differentiation lines. Thus, the link will occur by subtle and less subtle practices of exclusion—as we find in the fields of economic and social capital (see Bourdieu, 1988).

The Western reader of *the Chin-ssu lu* may try to reconstruct or interpret the *Chin-ssu lu* as a theory of *readiness to learn* (in the German tradition called *Bildsamkeit*, cf. Kühne, 1976). This may be considered a natural pattern. However, this motivational condition must be *cultivated*: significant educational efforts will usually aim at self-education (*Bildung*). Learning is the most important feature of self-cultivation—this can be regarded in the Chin-ssu lu as the crucial intuition of *implicit virtue ethics*.

Learning as self-cultivation and care for the self may be considered a *meta*-virtue: the virtue to become virtuous or a better person. This fundamental human motivation seems to be highly recognized in most cultures—for it appears to be the only way to escape from indifference, apathy, and despair prevalent in education culture today (Chin-ssu lu, II, 55, [1967, p. 63]).

Disclosure statement

No potential conflict of interest was reported by the author.

Notes

1. Edited in German by Wolfgang Ommerborn (2008).
2. To give one example: 'In Western philosophy, the question of "What is the Truth?" has taken a center stage. However, to the Confucian cultures, this question does not occupy a central position. The concept of truth is understood differently between the Western and the Confucian world. In the West, truth is knowledge of reality, basically representations of the world' (Kim, 2004, 118).
3. 'If a person is essentially sharp-witted but does not study, then he is really not sharp-witted' (Chu Hsi 1991, p. 93).
4. The *Classic of Changes* (early cosmological views), the *Book of Odes* (a compilation of over 300 odes, folk songs, ballads, court poetry, dynastic hymns ...), the *Book of History* (a collection of documents, speeches, and pronouncements on the theme of governance), the *Book of Rites* (a compendium of rituals and rules of etiquette), and the *Spring and Autumn Annuals* (a chronicle of events in the state of Lu, the native state of Confucius).
5. Without any doubt there is *positive pedagogical anthropology* in Confucian and Neo-Confucian thought: 'Know that human nature is originally good and hold with loyalty and faithfulness as fundamental. This is the way to build up, first of all, the noble part of your nature' (Chin-ssu lu, II, 70, [1967, p. 68]). The idea of the good nature of all human beings is, nevertheless, embedded in rather strict conceptions of social conventions. The importance of good relationships and sensitivity toward status distinctions is crucial: father and son, ruler and subject, husband and wife, old and young, and friend and friend, according to Mencius, had become the five paradigmatic relationships binding Chinese society together. In this context, Daniel Gardener has commented or guessed: 'Perhaps because goodness is relationship dependent, Confucius himself, although deeply preoccupied with virtue, never provides a comprehensive definition of it' (Gardener, 2007, p. 140).
6. The notion of *Bildung* does not however only refer to the process—as the formation or development of a person—but also to the result, the 'final shape'. *Bildung* is said to have an 'objective' and a subjective aspect. Whereas the former refers to 'culture' (as a philosophical, scientific, esthetic, moral, in short: 'reasonable' interpretation of the world, either referred to as *Allgemeine Menschenbildung* [general human education] or as *Allgemeinbildung* [broad educational experience]), the latter refers to the specific way of acquiring the objective content of culture in each case (ibid.). To that extent, we may say that what groups of humans perceive as culture (ethnicities, nations, communities, etc.) is *Bildung* at the level of the individual (von Hentig, 1985, p. 206).
7. This insight will become popular with the Piaget tradition in psychology and pedagogy, earlier in the work of Herbart, later Dewey (cf. English, 2013).

References

Bollenbeck, G. (1996). *Bildung und Kultur: Glanz und Elend eines deutschen Deutungsmusters* [Bildung and Culture: Splendor and Misery of a German Interpretative Model]. Frankfurt a.M.: Suhrkamp.

Bourdieu, P. (1988). *Die feinen Unterschiede. Zur Kritik der gesellschaftlichen Urteilskraft* [Distinction: A Social Critique of the Judgement of Taste]. Frankfurt a. M.: Suhrkamp.

Chu, H. (1991). *Further reflecions on things at hand. A reader, Zhu Xi.* Translation and Commentary by A. Wittenborn. Lanham a.o.: University Press of America.

Confucius. (1979). *The Analects (Lun yü)*. Translated with an introduction by D. C. Lau. London a.o.: Penguin.

De Bary, T. (1979). Introduction. In W. Theodore de Bary & I. Bloom (Eds.), *Principle and practicality. Essays in neo-Confucianism and practical learning* (pp. 1–33). New York, NY: Columbia University Press.

English, A. R. (2013). *Discontinuity in learning. Dewey, Herbart, and education as transformation.* Cambridge: Cambridge University Press.

Festinger, L. (1957). *A theory of cognitive dissonance.* Stanford, CA: Stanford University Press.

Fink, E. (1970). *Erziehungswissenschaft und Lebenslehre* [Educational Science and Life Philosophy]. Freiburg i. Br.: Rombach.

Foucault, M.u.a. (1993). *Technologien des Selbst* [Technologies of the Self] (mit Beiträgen v. R. Martin, L. H. Martin, W. E. Paden, H. Gutman, P. H. Hutton). Frankfurt a.M.: Fischer.

Gardener, D. K. (2007). *The four books. The basic teachings oft he later Confucian tradition.* Translation, with introduction and commentary, by D. K. Gardener. Indianapolis, IN: Hackett Publishing.

Hadot, P. (1996). Histoire du souci [The History of Care]. In *magazine littéraire*, Nr. 345, pp. 18–23.

Hadot, P. (1981). *Exercices spirituels et philosophie antique* [Spiritual Exercises and the Philosophy of Antiquity]. Paris: Études augustiennes.

Hon, T.-k. (2010). Zhou Dunyi's philosophy of the supreme polarity. In J. Makeham (Ed.), *Dao companion to neo-Confucian philosophy* (pp. 1–16). Dordrecht: Springer.

Hörster, R. (1995). Bildung. In H.-H. Krüger & W. Helsper (Eds.), *Einführung in Grundbegriffe und Grundfragen der Erziehungswissenschaft* [Introduction to Key Notions and Questions of Educational Sciences] (pp. 43–52). Opladen: Leske und Budrich.

Humboldt, W. v. (1969). Werke in fünf Bänden [Collected Works in five Volumes]. In hrsg. v. A. Flitner u. K. Giel. *Band IV Schriften zur Politik und zum Bildungswesen* [Volume IV Writings on Politics and the Educational System]. 2. durchges. Aufl. Darmstadt: Wissenschaftliche Buchgesellschaft.

Ivanhoe, P. J. (1993). *Confucian moral self cultivation.* New York, NY: Lang.

Jaspers, K. (1964). *Die massgebenden Menschen. Sokrates, Buddha, Konfuzius, Jesus* [Influential Persons: Socrate, Buddha, Confucius, Jesus]. München: Piper.

Kim K. H. (2004). An attempt to elucidate notions of lifelong learning: Analects-based analysis of Confucius' ideas about learning. *Asia Pacific Education Review*, 5, 117–126.

Koller, H.-C. (1999). *Bildung und Widerstreit. Zur Struktur biographischer Bildungsprozesse in der (Post-)Moderne* [Bildung and Conflict (Différence). The Structure of Biographical Processes in (Post-) Modernity]. München: Fink.

Kühne, J. (1976). *Der Begriff der Bildsamkeit und die Begründung der Ethik bei Johann Friedrich Herbart* [The Notion of Educationability and the Foundation of Ethics of Johann Friedrich Herbart]. Zürich: Juris.

Miller-Kipp, G. (1992). *Wie ist Bildung möglich? Die Bildung des Geistes unter pädagogischem Aspekt* [How is Bildung possible? The Education of the Mind from a Pedagogical Perspective]. Weinheim: Deutscher Studien Verlag.

Ommerborn, W. (Ed.). (2008). *Jinsilu. Aufzeichnungen des Nachdenkens über Naheliegendes. Texte der Neokonfuzianer des 11. Jahrhunderts*. Aus dem Chinesischen übersetzt und herausgegeben von W. Ommerborn. Frankfurt a.M.: Insel/Verlag der Weltreligionen.

Paul, G. (2006). Eine gültige Theorie der Kritik: Klassisch-gelehrte Ansätze in chinesischen Texten [A Valid Theory of Critique. Approaches in Classical Chinese Texts]. In H. Roetz (Ed.), *Kritik im alten und modernen China* (pp. 48–62). Wiesbaden: Harrassowitz Verlag.

Paul, G. (2010). *Konfuzius und Konfuzianismus* [Confucius and Confucianism]. Darmstadt: Wissenschaftliche Buchgesellschaft WBG.

Piaget, J. (1957). *Construction of reality in the child*. London: Routledge & Kegan Paul.

Platon. (1993). *Le souci du bien* [The Care for the Good]. Traduit du grec et presenté par Myrto Gondicas. Paris: arléa.

Platon. (1996). *Alcibiade* [Alcibiades]. Traduit par Maurice Croiset, revue par Marie-Laurence Desclos. Introduction et notes de Marie-Laurence Desclos. Paris: Les Belles Lettres.

Pleines, J.-E. (1971). *Die Pädagogische Bedeutung des Begriffs "Bildung"* [The Pedagogical Meaning of the Notion of Bildung]. Herausgegeben in: ders., Studien zur Bildungstheorie [Studies on the Theory of Bildung]. Darmstadt: Wissenschaftliche Buchgesellschaft, 1989, S. 7–62.

Pleines, J.-E. (1989). *Studien zur Bildungstheorie* [Studies on the Theory of Bildung]. Darmstadt: Wissenschaftliche Buchgesell-schaft.

Posner, H. (1988). Ist Bildung durch Wissenschaft heute noch ein realistisches Ziel? In F. Edding (Ed.), *Bildung durch Wissenschaft in neben- und nachberuflichen Studien* (pp. 22–37). Berlin: Max-Planck-Institut für Bildungsforschung.

Shun, K.-l. (2010). Zhu Xi's moral psychology. In J. Makeham (Ed.), *Dao companion to neo-Confucian philosophy* (pp. 177–196). Dordrecht: Springer.

Taylor, C. (1985). *Self-interpreting animals*. Philosophical papers, Bd. I: *Human agency and language*. Cambridge: Cambridge University Press, 1985, p. 45ff.

Taylor, C. (1989). *Sources of the self: The making of the modern identity*. Cambridge, MA: Harvard University Press.

Tweed, R. G., & Lehman, D. R. (2002). Learning considered within a cultural context. Confucian and Socratic approaches. *American Psychologist, 57*, 89–99.

von Hentig, H. (1985). *Die Menschen stärken, die Sache klären. Ein Plädoyer für die Wiederherstellung der Aufklärung* [Strengthen the Person, Clarifying the Subject Matter. A Plea for the Restoration of Enlightenment]. Stuttgart: Reclam jun.

Watson, P. (2010). *The German genius. Europe's third renaissance, the second scientific revolution and the twentieth century*. London a.o.: Simon & Schuster.

Wei-ming, T. (1979). *Humanity and self-cultivation: Essays in Confucian-thought*. Berkley, CA: Asian Humanities Press.

Zhu, X., & Lü, T.-C. (1967). *Reflections on things at hand (Chin-ssu lu)*. The neo-Confucian anthology compiled by Chu Hsi & Lü Tsu-Ch'ien. Translated, with notes, by Wing-Tsit Chan. London: Columbia University Press.

A Theory of Learning (学) in Confucian Perspective

CHUNG-YING CHENG

Abstract

In this article, I present a model of four dimensions for the idea of learning in the classical Confucian perspective. This model is intended to capture the most essential four aspects of learning which explain why self-cultivation of a human person toward an end of self-fulfillment and social transformation of humanity is possible. I shall also show how this model illuminates all basic uses of the term 'xue' (学, learning) in the Analects and thus leads to a more coherent understanding of the Confucian moral and ethical philosophy than have been previously done. A copingstone principle of sincerification is also suggested for enabling the advancement of a person to a higher status of life such as junzi (君子 a learned person) and shengxian (圣贤 sagely person).

A Four-Dimensional Model of Learning

We have to realize that the Chinese word 'xue' (学 learning) is used both as a noun and as a verb. Like many other Chinese words, 'xue' (学) is more a verb than a noun. The character suggests that a young person is doing study or learning something in a place. In this sense, 'xue' (学) as a verb has the status of an action or a process which is undertaken by a person. It is inevitably an action-dispositional property of the human person which enables a person to be more than what he is in a given state. If we distinguish between what is instinctually given and what is to be acquired, we have to say that 'xue' (学) is that power or action which would enable a person to acquire some skill or understanding or knowledge which is otherwise not instinctively given. But, we must also observe that *xue* (learning) is itself given as an instinct, which enables us to improve on our instincts or to add what is not given in instinct. We can learn many things from knowledge to skill, from strategy to tactics, even from truth to untruth or lie. This explains why the result of *xue* is not necessarily more powerful to *xue*, but something which may block one's ability to *xue*. In Mandarin Chinese, we speak of *xuehao* (学好 learn to be good) vs. *xuehuai* (学坏 learning to be bad). This leads to the question of the underlying intention of *xue* (学), which has a direct bearing on the end or result of the learning. We can learn how to survive or thrive. Why could someone not be capable of learning how to steal or how to rob or kill? There is no reason, why not. As Xunzi (荀子 298-238 BCE) would claim, what one learns reflects what one learns from. Thus, it is said that if one is close to the red paint, one becomes red, if one is close to a black paint, one becomes black.[1] This strongly suggests that the learning environment is the most important for the quality of learning and its result. It is no wonder why Mencius's mother has moved home three times in order to be sure about having the right neighborhood for the young Mencius (Mengzi 孟子 371-289 BCE) to learn.[2]

This observation should lead to a deeper insight into the nature of learning or *xue*: namely, *xue* is an action composed of two aspects for a person, the awakening or awareness of the mind and nature of the learner as pinpointed by Shouwen *Jiezi Wordbook* (说文解字) and *Kangxi Dictionary* (康熙字典), and the investigation and pursuit of knowledge of the object of learning in the mind of the learner as advocated by Zhu (朱熹 1130-1120). In either case, the idea of learning is linked to the idea of teaching, for teaching is a positive force which imposes or induces a change of the subject. It is through the influence of the object or environment of learning that the learner has acquired consciously or unconsciously a quality in one's mind or nature, so that the learner can be said to have interacted with the object or be influenced causally by it, whether he may be aware or not. But as we shall see, it is important that for Confucius, *xue* or learning should be made conscious and should be considered to be a self-consciously ingraining process from which one grows and advances in one's abilities and capabilities, especially in regard to acquisition and development of moral virtues, such as benevolence, justice, proprieties, and wisdom.

Based on our analysis of the word *xue* in the above, it is important for us to see that *xue* is a motor power for the growth and development of a human person by exposing the person to the world, so that he can become aware of and acquire a new capability or a new piece of knowledge in his life. In this sense, *xue* (learning) is a natural force which inheres in the existence of a human being in so far as he is a human being. In this sense, once a human being is born, he has the instinct to learn, so that he can come to know things in the world and himself. Here, we recall that Confucius says that if a person is born to know it is best, the next best is one who learns to know (*The Analects* 16-9). What Confucius has in mind is that it is rare that one could be *born* to know many things: there may be people who are born to be highly intelligent and could acquire knowledge without much effort, while most of us have to learn things with repeated effort and practice. Besides, one can be generally intelligent and is capable of learning one thing and then come to know more things by extension or by analogy. This is known as a method of using one illustration to reach three more by reflection (举一而反三). In this sense, a person 'born with knowledge' means that he could have more intuitive or intellectual power to achieve understanding and knowledge, but he still has to learn more if he wants to have extensive use of his knowledge or to preserve his insights for planning his future. Hence, 'to have knowledge at birth' (生而知之) must be a comparative statement on the quickness and easiness of learning to know, but does not mean to know without learning. For, we can indeed then claim that learning should include not only intuitive understanding or immediate understanding, but also the awakening of a learning disposition and a capability inherent in a person because of our general experience of life.

In this sense, we must also see learning as a matter of forming a concept or coming to a proposition regarding what Hume called matters of fact and relations of ideas, where ideas are already learned in a pre-understanding manner. Pre-understanding should not be conceived as having innate ideas or anything like that, but instead as having a naturally formed background of understanding from experience of things and natural reflection. For example, we learn to count three particular and discrete objects, and then we come to form the concretion of three which may appear to be independent of these three particular things, but which applies to any other particular collection of three things. Do we say that we have the innate and abstract knowledge of the three? If one child claims she knows what three is, how do we distinguish her concept of three from her ostensive perception on three things? It is through experience that we come to have concepts and it is through our application to experience that we know that we acquired concepts.

It is with this observation that we come to see that Shengzhi (生知, born to know) and Xuezhi (学知, learn to know) only differ in degrees in the facility of understanding in experience but are not qualitatively different. Learning is a process of knowing and we know by experience or reflection, not by the determination of given innate ideas. It is in this sense that Confucius stressed the importance of learning over all because, without learning as a motivating force and a force which would bring out what is dispositional and potential in terms of what we have learned, there would be no knowledge to be achieved, and consequently there would be no character to be molded and no virtue to be accomplished. One may raise the question as to whether, when Mencius speaks of the *liangzhi* (良知, intuitive knowledge), there is some form of innate knowledge of good, and therefore there could be some innate and *a prior* knowledge. This no doubt brings out an important consideration on learning: whether in the moral knowledge of good and bad there could be innate knowledge which does not depend on prior experience or learning. The fact is that the so-called *liangzhi* (良知, intuitive knowledge) is not a conceptual knowledge, even though we may form a theoretical concept of *liangzhi* from our reflection and analysis of what we have experienced in our feeling–responses to events and people in the world. As Mencius has described, 'The ability which we have and yet not have learned from outside is *liangneng* (良能); the knowledge which we have and yet not have considered on reflection is *liangzhi* (良知, intuitive knowledge).'[3] This statement clearly denies that there is a reflection involved for the knowledge we call *liangzhi*. This is not incompatible with my suggestion that *liangzhi* is not a conceptual knowledge but must be a dispositional faculty to perceive and think in a certain way.

The question is then: What is it that characterizes the way we perceive and think in a situation which we call *liangzhi* (良知)? As I have discussed this issue in a separate paper and responded to the questions relating to this issue,[4] my simple answer is that the perceiving and thinking of *liangzhi* in a person is always directed to a good value, and thus to a good end which contributes to our flourishing and our avoidance of harm in coherence with what we have known and with what we have experienced. It is therefore also an action-oriented perception and thinking, reflecting the close link or identity of the world, which I am perceiving as a good-producing power with what I have desired naturally. It is a complex situation of revealing my deep sense of care and hope in connection with the present situation or the world state.

The second factor for *liangzhi* is to do with an action and a decision to act. Once *liangzhi* (良知, intuitive knowledge) is activated and followed, we can be said to do the right thing, and the result of our action is expected to be in a good faith. Needless to say, even though it warrants an action to be morally significant and correct, it has no guarantee, however, that it must be productive of good and that yet it is itself intrinsically good. Now, this knowledge is to be contrasted with the knowledge we derive from our objective investigation. It is said in the text, the *Great Learning* (大学 *Daxue*), that we should investigate things for knowledge as the beginning of our self-cultivation. This investigation is required because we must know our environment in such a way that we can respond to it correctly. In other words, we must have knowledge of the world so that our *liangzhi* (良知, intuitive knowledge) can be enacted for correct orientation and with the right focus. If we do not have the world knowledge or we have insufficient knowledge of our environments, we may be misled and think of things which are not intended as we could naturally respond to a reality of which we are a part.

If what we may respond to is not a reality of which we form a part, we will become seriously harmed or seriously harming, just as a person steps on an illusionary step or pushes an imagined door, and in doing so, falling out of a stair way or fall into a pit. In the case of seeing the wrong person, our action could be most inappropriate and uncalled for. With this said, we see how our knowledge by investigation is the ground and basis for our *liangzhi* (intuitive knowledge), so that we may say that in order for our action to be correct, our *liangzhi* has to act on a learning process of investigation of things and formation of knowledge which are applicable to a reality. This means that the latter must be presupposed for the former and they together form a union of theory and practice. It is clearly indicated in *the Great Learning* (the *Daxue*) that the so-called 格物致知, that is, the acquisition of knowledge by investigation of things, must give rise to the making true or sincerifying of intentions (诚意) and the rectification of heart–mind (正心), the union of which in my interpretation is equivalent to the obtaining of the *liangzhi* (intuitive knowledge). If we see this connection between '诚意正心' and '良知', (*liangzhi*) we may in fact come to the position that they refer to the same ultimate ontological reality from which we originate as a human being. To return to this reality as the source of the reality of the human existence is the meaning of sincerety (cheng 诚) or truth-making. To make true our intentions (*chengyi* (诚意) or sincerefication) means to return to the reality, from which we may derive a power of assertion and action which transforms. This is what the knowledge of good in a process of actualization of *liangzhi* is about. In the text, *the Doctrine of the Mean* (中庸 Zhong Yong), Zisi (子思 in late fifth century BCE) comes to speak of the mutual entailment of 诚 (sincerity) and 明 (clear understanding and clarity) which illustrates how *liangzhi* (intuitive knowledge) can be said to be a matter of intuitive moral knowledge as it is illuminated by our sincere and clear mind.[5] We must assume that once we have *liangzhi*, we would also have *liangzhi* as a native capability to fulfill what we will and desire in light of our understanding.

The important point is that there are two stages of learning: the first stage of learning as learning of the knowledge of the world and the second stage of learning as learning of the right way of action based on the first stage of learning. The second stage is called the action of 'fulfilling the *liangzhi*' (致良知) or attaining *liangzhi* in a process of relating and endeavoring, which is also the process of making oneself sincere in reality and setting one's mind in the right direction.[6]

There is one final consideration about *xue* (学 learning) which we need to explore. We need to explore what the achievement of learning is expected and looked for in the Confucian enterprise of learning. It is clear that if a Confucian philosopher is simply looking for knowledge of things, he can acquire such knowledge by the investigation of things. From Confucius to Neo-Confucian philosophers in the Song and Ming Periods of Chinese history, very few Confucian scholars seem to be satisfied with or merely devoted to learning by the investigation of things; they all want to go beyond the learning of things to achieve the knowledge of people, rites (moral proprieties), and even language arts. Confucius himself makes this point: 'If one does not know the mandate (of heaven), one would not become a self-ruling person (*junzi* 君子). If one does not know rites, one would not establish oneself. If one does not know language, one would not be able to know others.'[7]

It is clear that in order to know *ming* (命 mandate, here meaning the mandate of heaven or 天命 *tianming*), to know rites (礼), and to know language (言), we have to know the facts about the mandate, the rites, and the people, and thus to know these objects as objects of our feelings and understanding, so that we can practice them in our life. For the latter, one needs to know what is embodied in those facts about these objects; it is, in other words, to know the feelings and spirit behind the facts about these things. This knowledge involves a dimension of ourselves which is not to be derived by observation, but to be established by reflection and deep experience of the human self. Hence, one can see how the knowledge of people, heaven, and language and even poetry must be acquired by ourselves as reflective entities in our minds. It is in this sense that this knowledge is the knowledge of other people by reflection of myself and by extension of one's own heart–mind to the heart–minds of others. *It is then not knowledge from learning by investigation but knowledge from learning by reflection.* This knowledge and learning are interactive and communicative because they link two or more heart–minds on the level of understanding and sharing. Besides, this knowledge and learning are also transformative and uplifting. How so? It is because in acquiring knowledge from another mind or from ourselves, we become more aware of ourselves as an ethical person and a moral agent. We will have developed our virtues as some conscious dispositions or as dispositions which would enable us to be free from prejudices and selfishness and to make judgments independently of ourselves as mere physical bodies. This means that learning on the higher level or the second level is axiologically oriented and spiritually directed.

In light of the above, we come to see our learning as a way of achieving the transformation of oneself and others as well as a way of fulfilling ourselves and others as we come to learn that everyone has a heart–mind and a nature, and our heart–mind needs to become free and creative, while our natures all require to be cultivated. In light of the present analysis, the self-cultivation of a person has two horizontal dimensions of learning which are the awakening of oneself, on the one hand, and understanding others and reality, on the other. Similarly, the self-cultivation of a person has also two vertical dimensions of learning, which are the realization of knowledge by investigation and the realization of knowledge by reflection. Of course, in these two processes, we see learning becomes differentiated into learning different virtues, and also simultaneously becomes integrated into a system of one principle ('My way is penetrated with oneness').[8]

Therefore, we come to a scheme of learning issues in the following:

Learning of Knowledge by reflection
Awakening from inside xue (学, learning) Influence from outside
Learning of Knowledge by investigation

In this presentation, we can easily see how 'awakening from inside' can be described as a spirit of self-knowledge, whereas the influence from outside can be described as a spirit of seeking objective truth. Similarly, we may describe the learning of knowledge by investigation as the learning of the basic (下学), and the learning of knowledge by reflection as the learning of the ultimate (上达) which can be said to consist of the way of the heaven (天道) and possibly also the mandate of heaven (天命).[9] We may indeed argue that as the learning of the basic would lead to the learning of the ultimate by way of reflection, our gained understanding of the ultimate may also illuminate our learning of the basic and this eventually leads to the importance of 'dedicating ourselves to the *dao* (the Way)' (志于道).[10]

How Learning is Understood in *the Analects*

There are a count of 66 '*xue*' words (学 learning) in *the Analects*. This is less than the number of the '*ren*' word (仁 humanity and benevolence). But there is no doubt that Confucius takes *xue* to be central to a human person, not only a *junzi* (the learned person) or a *shengxian* (the sagely person).[11] *Xue* is the basis and source for becoming a human person, a *junzi*, and a *shengxian*. As I have pointed out, *xue* as a disposition is instinctive and yet it is also reflective in that we must go beyond our instincts to learn. We can then regard *xue* as a methodology or skill for advancing us to a higher level of being, but can indeed advance a whole society or the world to a higher level of existence, in terms of knowledge and morality. That is why Confucius takes *xue* very seriously by speaking of: 'If we learn and often review what we learn, is it a great joy?'[12]

Learning makes one to grow up and be exposed to new things and even new challenges, but it is always a joy to grow and be able to solve problems of life. Of course to review old knowledge is also fun, for it provides a chance to make new things out of the old as we have always known. Besides, we can correct our errors and revise our old knowledge by looking into it time and again through our new experience and new reflection.

THE CONFUCIAN CONCEPT OF LEARNING

After certain periods of life, we tend to expend our life more than to build our life because the task of living would always burden us with the demands of life and social obligations, and other pressures of life situations. How much time do we have or have left to seek learning or to refresh our hearts and minds to creatively grow and freely exercise our faculties, and therefore to experience the pure joys of life? Not too much. To say this is not to ignore, but rather to accentuate the need to learning for the purpose of upgrading our life. This means that we need to take learning to be an opportunity for integrating and advancing our life to a higher stage and a deeper understanding. Thus, we read what Confucius says about the advance of his own life at some time after becoming 70 years old: 'I have devoted myself to learning at 15. At 30 I have established my self. At 40 I have achieved a mind of freedom from doubts. At 50 I came to know the mandate of heaven. At 60 I became pliant with ears. At 70 I can follow the wishes of my heart and mind without trespassing any moral rules.'[13] Given this account of his life, we have to be assured that this age transformation is a result of stage integration based on learning. It comes to a point where Confucius can say that 'My way is penetrated with oneness' (吾道一以贯之).[14] Following this, I appreciate Zixia's comment: 'The *junzi* (君子, a learned man) reaches the *dao* (the Way) by learning' (君子学以致其道).[15]

But then, we must ask the question: On what kind the methodology of learning is involved in this process of moral transformation and development of one's mind? I raise this question because we must beware of the distinction between *xue* as an end and *xue* as a means. It is clear that Confucius takes the cultured forms of human expression and language seriously, which is what he has referred to as the polished form or *wen* (文). *Wen* is also the shared knowledge and values of humanity which should temper a human's raw desires and uncivilized nature. Hence, to know *wen* is to know the results of learning from a tradition, which is what imbues a human person with a sense of order and reason. On this basis, one must develop the *li* or rites (礼) for social and moral living. Hence, one way of understanding the methodology of learning is to understand learning as consisting in the broad attainment of knowledge and that of the restraint of the *li* or rules of behavior. That is why Confucius says: '博学以文, 约之以礼.'[16] On the other hand, there is a better and complete description of this methodology which consists of theory and practice. It is found in the text of *the Doctrine of Mean* (the Zhongyong): 'Wide learning, careful questioning, clear distinction, serious thinking and sincere practice' (博学之, 审问之, 慎思之, 明辨之, 笃行之).[17] In these five steps of learning methodology, we can see that learning is bound up with thinking and practice. It is not simply an empty talk but must be the engagement of mind. Hence, Confucius says: 'Learning without thinking leads to perplexity; thinking without learning gives rise to weariness.'[18]

Given our four-dimensional model of learning, learning must involve a reference to the reality as well as to the activities of mind. The interaction between the two must lead to the awakening of heart and mind to a deeper level of reality, as this reality would become illuminated by the mind or embodied by the heart. As mind and heart cannot be separable, even though distinguishable, in their corresponding activities, there is an underlying unity between the two, which can be identified as the nature (性) that is itself rooted in the way of heaven (天道). But the methodology we just encountered may not recognize the two levels of reality, the way of Heaven (天道) and the nature (性), even though Confucius may not explicitly speak of them in *the Analects*.[19] However, as we see from the beginning section of *the Doctrine of Mean* (the Zhong Yong), we come to see how it is the nature of man which must be identified from its origination of the way of heaven. In order to understand the nature of man, perhaps we can either take the Kantian position, by describing the nature of man as transcendentally warranted by an idea of an unconditioned source, or take the Heideggerian position (also Xiong Shili-like position), by recognizing the disclosure or presentation of a deep root of the human nature. By understanding learning as a process of awakening and a process of recognition, it seems reasonable to see that it is through learning that we come to know, possibly to fulfill, our nature and to gain an insight or experience the reality of the heaven's way as the source and root of our nature. We may in fact come to appreciate how Confucius can be described as a person of 'tireless learning and never weary teaching' (学而不厌、教而不倦).[20]

In regard to what learning can bring to a person, it is important to keep in mind that what makes a person more cultivated is his virtues. Virtues are the vehicles for one's humanity and the way in which one will achieve a better or a more genuine personality. Keeping this in mind, one might wish to say that the main end for learning is to enable a person to become virtuous, so that his life will become meaningful and his personhood will become valuable, for he will then become a self-ruling person (*junzi* 君子), which is the basis for becoming a sage (圣贤). One's doubt needs to be dispersed in the very beginning. In speaking of the end of learning as becoming a *junxi* (君子) or even a *shengxian* (圣贤), we do not mean that we can learn to become a *junzi* or *shengxian* just in the same way as we learn to become a carpenter or a car driver, which involves the learning of a skill. It is of course not that we are capable of learning all kinds of techniques or skills because each skill requires special training and adaptation. It is not that all people are suitable for such training or capable of such adaptation. In training to become an astronaut, we need to have certain physical capabilities and conditions which may not be shared by all people. But once we meet those conditions and have those capabilities, it is likely that we can be trained to become an astronaut. On the other hand, as Mencius maintains, all people can become a sage (圣贤). It is also assumed that all men can become a self-ruling man (*junzi*, 君子). To become a *shengzian* or a *junzi*, one needs to learn to open one's mind and heart to have the aspiration or desire and will (*zhi* 志) to become one and to have an ideal or model for such character transformation or uplifting. He would also emulate and aspire to endeavor toward such an ideal as Confucius. But doing all of these does not mean that a person would ignore small details of training one's self to be capable of suffering, tolerating, courageous, and knowledgeable. This means again that to learn to become a *junzi* or *shengxian*, one needs to be attentive to many factors of body and mind, feeling and will, far more than in the case of becoming a skilled person. But on the other hand, a *junzi* or *shengxian* need not to be a skilled person, even though he may be indeed a skilled person, like being a good carpenter or a driver. In this sense, we can see how learning to be a *junzi* or a *shengxian* is conceived: it is a matter of overall transformation of the personality of a person with no special skill to be absolutely required. What is required, however, are the virtues one come to have, among which the most important one is to be benevolent or ren (仁) from which other virtues will ensue with regard to different dispensations and functions of humanity in sociality. Thus, we shall have righteousness (义), propriety (礼), wisdom (智), trustworthiness (信), and other related or auxiliary virtues, such as loyalty (忠) or filial piety (孝).

Although we see no absolute principle for learning to be a *junzi*, I would argue that the four-dimensional model provides a scheme and foundation for such learning. As we have seen, learning requires the participation of oneself in one's open mind being awakened to a new level of reality. Learning also requires a response to reality which is outside us to which we should pay our attentiveness. Learning further requires the knowledge of the world and the understanding of values and norms or ideals based on such knowledge; this means 'the integration of the inner and the outer' (合内外之道) as the *Doctrine of Mean* (the Zhong Yong) maintains. Although these four dimensions would provide a way of approach to the understanding of learning to be a *junzi* or a *shengxian* in so far as their virtues are concerned, we may wish to establish an overall principle which gives a meaning to the level of organic unity and creativity of the personality of a *juzi* or *shengxian* which is not confined to any specialty. Thus, Confucius has said: 'The *junzi* does not reside in being a utensil' (君子不器).[21]

We may indeed propose the self-grounding principle of sincerifying (*cheng* 诚) from *the Zhong Yong* and *the Mencius* to be the source and motivation for learning to become a *junzi* or *shengren*, i.e. to be the source for all virtues, especially for the source virtue of *ren* (仁).[22] Recall our understanding of sincerifying (*cheng* 诚) as seeking to return to the source of reality of the cosmic creativity. It is in the cosmic creativity of the ultimate reality from which one finds inspiration and the ever-sustaining effort and will to improve oneself to refine and to perfect or complete oneself. If a person is not sincere and fails to found his life on the ultimate reality of cosmic power, how does he maintain his own reality or the truthfulness of his language and the validity of his conduct and action? This is perhaps the most important insight of all the Confucian scholars to seek to reach, and establish sincerity as a matter of making one's own life genuine. In this sense, we speak of 'There is nothing if there is no sincerity' (不诚无物) and 'The utmost sincerity is divinelike' (至诚如神).[23] It is this creative source which gives us a power for sustenance and even an intelligence to seek to become a *junzi* and then a *shengxian*, which means to accomplish oneself in order to accomplish others (成己以成人).

The power of sincerety (诚) is clearly illustrated in the following words of *the Zhong Yong*:

诚者，天之道也；诚之者，人之道也。诚者不勉而中，不思而得，从容中道，圣人也。诚之者，择善而固执者也[24]

As we see, it is from this establishing of 诚, 立诚, in oneself that one can then proceed to the methodology of learning as indicated in the Zhong Yong words '博学之, 审问之, 慎思之, 明辨之, 笃行之.' It requires a perceptive subtlety in a person to see that the '之' refers to precisely the creativity of the cosmic reality one would embody in going to the source of one's life and existence. But then, the most urgent question to ask is how one comes to reach for such sincerity as the original source of creativity? Mencius responds by saying 'to become sincere by reflection on oneself (反身而诚)'. But what is 'to become sincere by reflection on oneself?' In the discourse of *the Mencius*, the answer is simply that one needs to remove all obstacles and pollutions or coverings, so that one's original mind or nature will naturally and spontaneously spring out. This is what Mencius has referred to as 'the mind should not forget the goal nor make things to grow (心毋忘，毋助长也)'.[25]

However, in the text of *the Zhong Yong*, we have a different suggestion; it suggests that '顺乎亲有道，反诸身不诚，不顺乎亲矣。诚身有道，不明乎善，不诚乎身矣。'[26] Here, we see the attention is to be called to the understanding of the good or the end value of one's life. It implies the knowledge and integration of our experiences toward a goal based on the basic learning. This approach may not differ much from the opening sentence *of the Great Learning*: '大学之道，在明明德，在亲民，在止于至善。' In light of these two approaches, we must conclude that the best way for realizing the 诚 and going back to the creative source of reality by 诚 is to combine the internal with the external. We need to know the world and ourselves all together and integrate our experiences and reflections to a deeper root of understanding, from which a creative power as the creative source of reality would naturally spring out. *With this being said, the four-dimensional model still applies, but it can be capstoned with the integrative principle of sincerification as the ultimate principle and foundation or fountain of ceaseless learning.*

Concluding Remarks

Three observations need to be made with regard to how learning may also guard virtues not to be diminished or downgraded in time, in one's practice. Confucius says: '好仁不好学，其蔽也愚；好知不好学，其蔽也荡；好信不好学，其蔽也贼；好直不好学，其蔽也绞；好勇不好学，其蔽也乱；好刚不好学，其蔽也狂。'[27] As we analyze the nature of each virtue, we see that the virtue is attained as a mean or a balanced harmony between two extremes, and therefore needs learning or knowledge to maintain or achieve the balance. As a matter of fact, it is not simply learning as knowledge, but learning as an open attitude and a reflective receptivity, and thus modesty to achieve any balance. Even in the case of loving *ren* or indulging in practice *ren*, there is the risk of overdoing it when righteousness is called for, and therefore overdoing it may result in foolish or unintelligible decisions. This need for a balance and self-restraint in practicing a virtue requires, therefore, learning as both knowledge and open-mindedness to make it continue, sustain, and even present itself as virtue. Once one loses one's natural balance, balance provided by learning, one also loses sincerity and reality for that matter. In this regard, the importance of learning cannot be underestimated.

The second observation is: Confucius has also pointed out that once one's intelligence has reached a virtuous decision, one also needs to pay attention to the basic virtue of *ren* (仁), so that one's virtuous decision or action can be said to be rooted in humanity, and therefore will not lose itself for want of humanity. Further on, one needs an attitude of respect and should follow the propriety in order to finally achieve a good result or simply goodness. It is said that '知及之，仁不能守之，虽得之，必失之。知及之，仁能守之，不庄以莅之，则民不敬。知及之，仁能守之，庄以莅之，动之不以礼，未善也。'[28]

THE CONFUCIAN CONCEPT OF LEARNING

One last consideration concerns whether one must serve the government once one has attained a high degree of learning as the saying '仕而优则学, 学而优则仕' suggests.[29] If we regard serving the government as one way, and perhaps, sometimes the most needed or the best way of serving the people and humanity, there is no reason why one does not want to serve the government as a learned scholar. But Zixia's point is reciprocal, for he in fact speaks of '仕而优则学,' by which he means that one needs to take what remainder time is left from one's service for learning. This is no doubt significant, as it suggests that one should make an effort to enrich and strengthen oneself not only in the learning of useful knowledge for one's service, but also in learning for achieving and maintaining one's life status as a *junzi* in aspiration toward complete and ideal virtues.

Disclosure statement

No potential conflict of interest was reported by the author.

Notes

1. See the Writings of Xunzi, Chapter one 劝学篇.
2. This story about Mencius is often told as we read the 三字经.
3. See the Mencius, 尽心上。.
4. See my article on 'Creativity and Unity in the Philosophy of Wang Yangming:', in *Philosophy East and West,* Vol 23, No. 1–2, 1973. 49–72
5. See Zhong Yong, section 21.
6. Mencius speaks of 良知良能 in connection with his theory of human nature 性. It is in light of the experience of the 良知良能 he argues that human nature is good. This goodness of human nature is to be conceived as a consequence, not simply as a motivation.
7. The Analects, 20.3.
8. In this description of functions of learning, we come to see learning as both an end and a means for the development and transformation of the human being, as learning is a process of such development and transformation.
9. We need more explanation on this matter. How does Confucius come to know the mandate of heaven by the age of 50? It must be a reflective thinking which integrates the world experience he has gone through and his soul-searching for significance of his life just as he would ask the question of the 'significance of virtue' (德义) in the divination judgment in Zhouyi (see the Silk Manuscript '易之义'). As to knowing the way of heaven, it is a concept which requires again integration of our experience of the heaven and earth and the revealed meaning of the activities of heaven and earth. It can be said to be a deep insight of the creative power and purpose of the ultimate which represents our wisdom.
10. See the Analects 7.6. We may naturally have a sense of direction and end of life, but to be directed to the truth of the dao requires an understanding of the dao which cannot be achieved by way of learning in the sense of learning as indicated in my Confucian model of learning.
11. This has to be argued on the basis of my model of learning, for without learning in this sense, we cannot become even a junzi, not to say shengxian. It is on this model we can also see that every human being is capable of becoming a shengxian, as Mencius has argued.
12. See Analects, 20.3.
13. See the Analects 2.4.
14. See the Analects 15.2.
15. See the Analects 19.7. 子夏 also says that '博学而笃志, 切问而近思, 仁在其中矣' (ibid.,19.6) It is clear that it is through xue that we are able to solidify our aspirations

and seek answers to our queries on things at hand. It is in this manner we become caring for humanity, as we begin our benevolent care by reflecting on things close to us.
16. See the Analects 12.14.
17. See the Zhong Yong section 20.
18. See the Analects 2.15.
19. In the Analects, Confucius seldom addresses to 性与天道. But, he did speak of 性 and 天 and has not offered any speculation on 性与天道, except making some observation on human nature.
20. See the Analects 7.2. Mencius also mentioned this in his 公孙丑上.
21. See the Analects 2.12.
22. I make out a verb from the English word 'sincere' in consideration of the active nature of cheng 诚, which is translated into the English word 'sincere'. Hence, the verb form 'sincerify' is to make true.
23. See Zhong Yong sections 24, 25.
24. See Zhong Yong section 20.
25. See the Mencius 公孙丑上.
26. See the Zhong Yong Section 20.
27. See the Analects 17.8.
28. See the Analects 15.15.
29. See the Analects 19.13.

References

Daxue & Zhongyong (大学 & 中庸). (2012). Translated by Ian Johnston and Wang Ping. Hong Kong: The Chinese University Press.
Instructions for Practical Living and Other Neo-Confucian Writings by Wang Yang-Ming (传习录). (1963). Translated by Wing-Chit Chan. New York, NY: Columbia University Press.
Learning to Be a Sage: Selections from the Conversations of Master Chu (朱子语类). (1990). Translated by Daniel K. Gardner. Berkeley: University of California Press.
The Analects (论语). (2008). Translated with an introduction and notes by Raymond Dawson. Oxford: Oxford University Press.
The Mencius (孟子). (2004). Translated with an introduction and notes by D.C. Lau. London: Penguin.
Xunzi: the complete text (荀子). (2014). Translated and with an introduction by Eric L. Hutton. Princeton, NJ: Princeton University Press.
'Yizhuan (易传)' in *I-Ching: The Book of Change* (周易). (2015). Translated by David Hinton. New York, NY: Farrar, Straus and Giroux.

The Corporeality of Learning: Confucian Education in Early Modern Japan

MASASHI TSUJIMOTO

Abstract

The intellectual foundation of early modern Japan was provided by Confucianism—a system of knowledge set forth in Chinese classical writings. In order to gain access to this knowledge, the Japanese applied reading markers to modify the original Chinese to fit the peculiarities of Japanese grammar and pronunciation. Confucian education started by having the children memorize these Japanese readings (kundoku) of the Chinese classics by endless recitation (sodoku). This article will examine the significance of this study method in order to demonstrate the following: 1. The recitation of the Chinese classics led to these texts being 'incorporated' into the body, where they become the 'intellectual language' of thought and speech. 2. This quality of 'incorporation' was appreciated because it fostered the unity of thought and behavior, leading to the formation of a strong-willed subject. 3. This idea of 'incorporation' stands in stark contrast to the modern conception of knowledge that stresses objectivity and transparency, and ignores the pedagogical significance of the body.

1. Introduction

Confucianism was the intellectual foundation of early modern Japan (Edo period, 1603–1868). As the period's most orthodox system of knowledge and learning, all intellectual activity took place within the conceptual framework and specific terminology of Confucianism, and consequently, the mastery of Confucian knowledge was the precondition to any form of scholarly pursuit. In this article, I would like to focus upon the acquisition process of Confucian knowledge in order to grasp more fully the significance of this intellectual dominance to the nature and characteristics of elite knowledge in the period.

Basically, Confucianism is a kind of scholarly learning that specializes in reading the classical Chinese texts of the Confucian canon. These Classics, 13 in all, were taken either to be compiled by Confucius or to faithfully transmit the lives and teachings of Confucius and the Sages. As such, they were held to be sacred scriptures containing 'truth'—truth that could be revealed through relentless and meticulous study of their content—and Confucian scholars have labored through the centuries to clarify the meaning of the Classics by piling commentary upon commentary. Since all new intellectual endeavors were mediated by, and justified through, new interpretations of these sacred texts, we might even go as far as to say that the history of these commentaries is nothing other than the history of East Asian thought itself.

One of the educational consequences of this emphasis on the Classics is that the same texts are read, over and over, by both the beginning and advanced student. To be sure, the mode in which these texts were read differed according to age and ability, but the main curriculum stayed the same even over a lifetime of study. Whereas children would start their studies by phonetically reciting (*sodoku* 素読) texts such as the *Classic of Filial Piety* (*Xiaojing* 孝経) or the *Great Learning* (*Daxue* 大学), an advanced scholar would still be reading the same works, but now with a focus on the details of their correct interpretation. Unthinkable though, such a curriculum might be from the perspective of modern education, it was the pedagogy most suited to the single ultimate aim of Confucianism, namely to read and understand the Classics.

2. Confucian Texts in Seventeenth-Century Japan

2.1. Imported Books from China

Confucian learning in the seventeenth century was mostly accessed through the interpretations of Zhuxi 朱熹. As the official orthodox interpretation, Zhuxi's commentaries were the standard by which the civil service examinations of both China and Korea were graded, and as such, all those who aspired to a government position had no choice but to learn his ideas by heart. Zhuxi's commentary on the Four Books, the *Sishu jizhu* 四書集註 [Collected Commentaries on the Four Books] thus became a serious object of study itself, leading to the production of commentaries that sought to clarify it. Zhuxi's status is well illustrated by the fact that the Yongle 永楽 emperor himself ordered the compilation of the *Sishu daquan* 四書大全 [Complete Compendium on the Four Books] (publ. 1415), a 36-volume work that collected the most important interpretations of Zhuxi's commentaries. In effect, Confucian knowledge was not so much approached through the Classics themselves, but rather through Zhuxi's *Sishu jizhu* or more accurately still, through the commentaries thereof.

When Confucianism was reintroduced in Japan in the early seventeenth century, it was mediated by this Zhuxi learning. Not yet having a blossoming native print industry, the Japanese in this period were still largely dependent on Chinese and Korean imports for their knowledge of Confucianism, and so naturally came to share these countries' focus and respect for the *Sishu jizhu*, thereby becoming a member of the Sinosphere (*higashi ajia jukyōken* 東アジア儒教圏). This common approach to Confucian knowledge becomes apparent when we consider, for example, the case of Kaibara Ekiken 貝原益軒 (1630–1714), a Confucian scholar from Fukuoka domain who in his commentary on the *Sishu jizhu* cites a great variety of Ming commentaries on Zhuxi's work.

Most Japanese Confucians in this period, therefore, studied Confucianism mediated by commentaries to the *Sishu jizhu*, a trend that is emphasized by the exception-to-the-rule in the person of Yamazaki Ansai 山崎闇斎 (1618–1682), whose vehement criticism of his colleagues' reliance on secondary and recycled commentaries serves to illustrate the dominance of this kind of Zhuxi learning.

2.2. Adding Reading Marks to the Classics

To the Japanese, the imported books that arrived from China and Korea represented 'illegible texts' written in the foreign language of classical Chinese. Their scholarly mission, therefore, was inherently one of translation, that is, one of devising ways to make these foreign texts readable in Japanese. The tool that was used for this purpose was *kunten* 訓点, special reading marks to indicate word order, punctuation, and pronunciation in Japanese.

Much of this early translating work was done by Hayashi Razan 林羅山 (1583–1657), a *bakufu*-appointed Confucian scholar who had made it one of his missions to provide reading marks to those books from the Nagasaki import cargo list that he regarded as particularly useful. Razan's method of marking—that is, his interpretations—became widely known and used as *dōshunten* 道春点, Dōshun marks, named after his clerical name of Dōshun. Razan's pioneering efforts were then continued by the next generation of scholars such as Kaibara Ekiken, Nakamura Tekisai 中村惕斎 (1629–1701), Andō Seian 安東省庵 (1622–1701), and Mōri Teisai 毛利貞斎 (dates unknown), who each produced different versions of Chinese texts marked according to their respective interpretations.

3. Japanese Reprints and the Spread of Study Manuals for Confucian Learning

3.1. The Appearance of Japanese Reprints

The books imported from China and Korea were extremely costly and circulated only in small numbers among the aristocrat and warrior elite and the Confucian and Buddhist scholars who enjoyed their patronage. The development of ever-better Japanese printing techniques during the seventeenth century, however, would soon bring an end to this monopoly of knowledge.

Although the commercial print industry had started in Kyoto with the publication of handbooks of popular and practical knowledge, before too long, production had expanded geographically to Osaka and Edo, and topically to include a wide variety of popular and scholarly literature, including the so-called Japanese reprints (*wakokubon* 和刻本) or Chinese philosophical works with Japanese reading marks. Although these kinds of works had been produced in low numbers in earlier periods as well, their use had been restricted to a small readership of monks and local warlords. Now, however, these works were sold commercially to anyone who could afford them.

The demand for Japanese reprints was high enough to sustain the commercial production of a high variety of works such as the *Sishu daquan* (publ. 1630) and the *Zhuzi yulei* 朱子語類 [Recorded Sayings of Master Zhu] (publ. 1688). These reprints did not merely cater to a growing readership of Confucians, but they also—by virtue of ever lower prices—disseminated Confucian knowledge beyond the bounds of professional scholars, breaking the knowledge monopoly of the elite and creating an intellectual middleclass.

3.2. Study Manuals

Japanese reprints were first published with reading marks as minimal aids to reading, but as the market for Confucian knowledge grew, even more easily accessible texts were published. These study manuals (*gakushūsho* 学習書) circumvented the need for reading marks by simply rewriting the text in Japanese and often providing helpful reading tools such as glossaries and source references.

A good example of this genre of works is Nakamura Tekisai's *Shisho jimō kuge* 四書示蒙句解 [A Phrase by Phrase Explication of the Four Books for Beginning Students] (28 fasc.) published in 1719. This publication features the original text of the Four Books printed in large bold characters with the commentary of Zhuxi inserted in small double columns written in a mixture of Chinese characters and Japanese *katakana* syllabic script. According to its foreword, the work was published in response to a repeatedly expressed request for a printed version of Tekisai's lectures to his students. The target audience was likely the beginning student who could not read Zhuxi's *Sishu jizhu* in the original, but nonetheless, had the ambition to learn about its interpretations. The text uses accessible language and gives the impression that one is attending one of Tekisai's lectures in person.

Mōri Teisai's *Shisho shitchū rigen shō* 四書集註俚諺鈔 [The Sishu Jizhu Explained in Easy Language] (50 fasc. Publ. 1715)[1] is similar to Tekisai's work in that it offers a Japanese explanation to the original text and Zhuxi's interpretation, but adds the novelty of supporting the author's interpretations with references from a variety of Ming commentaries, those contained in the *Sishu daquan* as well as 20 other works. The variety and volume of these references, as well as the fact that they are cited in the original Chinese, while providing scholarly quality, also required a high level of Confucian knowledge on part of the reader. We can, therefore, surmise that it was aimed at advanced students who, while not completely satisfied with the level of Tekisai's instruction, were not capable of navigating the vast realm of Ming scholarship on their own, for example, teachers of Confucian schools in the more rural areas.

4. The Study Process of Confucian Learning

4.1. The Method of Sodoku

The most fundamental method of study within Confucianism is that of *sodoku*, or phonetic recitation, the aim of which is to commit the Classics to memory by repeatedly reading them aloud. The age that was regarded as the most suitable to begin *sodoku* was about seven or eight, a fact reflected in the age of matriculation in domain schools; 44% of students enrolled at age eight and 19% at age seven.[2] As to the method and results of effective *sodoku*, Kaibara Ekiken remarked as follows.

> One should recite a hundred characters of the Four Books every day, a hundred times, until you can read and write them by heart. (...) Once you have committed the Four Books to memory, you will come to grasp their meaning, thus enabling you to read other books with great ease. (...) After memorizing the Four Books, you have already completed half the task of a beginning scholar. (*Wazoku dōjikun* 和俗童子訓 [Precepts for Children in Colloquial Japanese]. (Kaibara, 1961))

Ekiken is making the point that *sodoku* provided a method for not merely memorizing texts, but also for acquiring the ability to read Chinese—an ability that then might be applied to reading other books. Although contemporary Chinese scholars recommended learning 300 characters per day, Ekiken lowers this number to a 100, in consideration of the fact that Japanese children would have no prior experience with the Chinese language. Nonetheless, even at this lower pace, it would be possible to go through the total of 52,804 characters that make up the Four Books in 528 days. Proceeding with the Six Classics would then take an extra four years to master, at which point, according to Ekiken, one would be able to read any kind of text.[3]

The teaching of *sodoku* took place on a one-on-one basis as opposed to uniform class instruction. The teacher and student would sit in front of each other with the text to be read in the middle facing the student. While indicating the characters one by one with his pointer (*jitsukibō* 字突棒), the teacher would read the text aloud for the student to repeat. Since perfect memorization is the ultimate aim of *sodoku*, if the student failed to memorize the text during class, he would continue to practice at home in order to master the relevant section by time of the next class. *Sodoku* thus involved short periods of intense instruction combined with long stretches of solitary repetition.

4.2. Lectures and Debates

After *sodoku*, the next step in Confucian education would be the lecture (*kōgi* 講義), through which meaning was provided to the large amount of texts that the student had committed to memory. According to Takeda Kanji, there are two levels of lecture to be distinguished. Students would start with the private lecture (*kōju* 講授), receiving one-on-one instruction from the teacher. In the sense that this method consists of short intensive instruction coupled with long periods of self-study, it can be considered an extension of *sodoku*. As the level of the student progressed, however, they would advance to class lectures (*kōshaku* 講釈), receiving uniform instruction together with other students (Takeda, 1969).

Lectures would be succeeded by group discussions (*kaigyō* 会業). These discussions took place in groups of about 10 students of equal ability and can be divided into two types: group readings (*kaidoku* 会読) and discussion circles (*rinkō* 輪講). Although both types place emphasis on student interaction through discussion, they differ slightly in their aims, and consequently, in their content and method. The main purpose of group readings is correct reading. To that end, students took turns in reading out passages from essential texts other than the Classics, such as histories (*shi* 史), philosophical works (*zi* 子), or literary works (*ji* 集). After one student had finished reading his passage aloud, the other students would correct his pronunciation and grammar mistakes.

In contrast, the discussion circle's aim was to explicate the Classics. On the basis of a variety of commentaries, students would argue orthodox and heterodox interpretations and try to establish the correct meaning of text passages. The sessions would be led by the most accomplished student, who would decide on the 'correct' answer in case of argument and sometimes assign grades to the students' performance as well. Since these discussions required thorough preparation in order for the students to participate effectively, the discussion circle can be said to provide the most rigorous practice for the task of being a Confucian scholar.

4.3. Text Scanning

Students would prepare for the seminar through a solitary and silent form of reading, namely text scanning (*kansho* 看書). The most important characteristic of this type of reading was not its solitary or silent nature, but rather the way in which it circumvented Japanese reading marks in order to allow for Chinese text to be read faster and more intuitively.

As professional readers, Confucians had to read in great variety and volume. On the basis of the diary of a certain domain scholar, for example, we know that they could spend about two hours every day reading some 200 pages of text (about 20.000 characters) (Fuchigami, 2009, p. 53). As it would be impossible to read an amount of Chinese like this while relying on Japanese reading marks—regardless of whether one reads the text aloud or not—it makes one wonder how the Japanese Confucians accomplished such a feat.

The answer lies in the way in which they had 'incorporated' (*shintaika* 身体化) a veritable database of text through the practice of *sodoku*. Through continuous repetition, hundreds of books, thousands of passages, and uncountable phrases had been etched into their minds, flesh, and bones, where they resided as the framework of thought and speech. Having been not merely memorized or internalized, but actually 'incorporated' into one's very physical being, these texts could be accessed instantly, and even unconsciously. Those who had gone through the *sodoku* process—that is, all Confucians—thus would be able to scan a Chinese text with their eyes and grasp its meaning intuitively without having to rely on Japanese grammar or pronunciation.

Ogyū Sorai 荻生徂徠 (1666–1728), a Confucian who passionately advocated accessing the Classics through the original language of Chinese, was also a proponent of this kind of scanned reading. To Sorai, scanned reading was the closest one could get to reading the classics as the Chinese would read them, leading him to the statement: 'Scanning books is superior to reading them.'

4.4. Poetry and Prose Composition

Apart from reading-based study practices—such as *sodoku*, lectures, and discussions—another valued exercise within Confucian education was that of composition of poetry and prose. To be sure, reading played an important preparatory role in these compositions as well; as in order to be able to create good poetry or prose, one first had to 'incorporate' the ancient models through *sodoku*. Nonetheless, once this process was completed, students would be required to go beyond the models and create their own works of poetry and prose.

The ability to use the classical Chinese language in order to write poetry and prose at will was a defining aspect of both the reputation and identity of early modern intellectuals. The reason why the Chinese language had come to monopolize intellectual production in this way is the result of the *sodoku* method, as I will explain in detail below.

5. Chinese as an Intellectual Language

5.1. The 'Incorporation' of Text

Since all scholarship in the early modern period was expressed in the classical Chinese language, scholars were required to not merely write and read, but to *think* in Chinese. As such, the most important challenge for beginning students of Confucianism was how to acquire full proficiency in this intellectual language. The method they adopted to this purpose, namely *sodoku*, is not necessarily an obvious choice. After all, why would the endless recitation of text—without even understanding its meaning—be expected to foster any kind of scholarly ability? To understand this problem, we need to realize that recitation was not the end goal, but merely the means to memorization. Or rather, it was the means to not merely committing the text to one's mind and memory, but to 'incorporating' it into one's physical being. By engaging one's eyes to read, one's ears to listen, and one's lungs and mouth to recite, *sodoku* involved a range of bodily senses and functions in order to etch a text permanently into the body of the student.

The result of this process of 'incorporation' was an intensely personal and direct communication with the sacred texts. Hearing a certain phrase of the Four Books would cause one to respond with the phrase that followed upon it, instantly and unconsciously, as if they were one's own words. In the sense that the Classics were records of the words and deeds of Confucius and the Sages, this meant that, effectively, one could speak and think in their language, and actually *embody* their principles and teachings.

5.2. The Japanese Reading of Chinese

The language used in *sodoku* was not the original Chinese, but a version of it that, through the aid of reading markers indicating word order and pronunciation, was modified to fit the peculiarities of Japanese grammar.[4] This 'Japanese reading' (*kundoku* 訓読) differs from both the spoken and written forms of the Japanese language, and might best be described as a strong and masculine variant of the written court language (*gago* 雅語) used by the imperial dynasty during the Heian period.

The reason that this very unique language was adopted for *sodoku* surely has to do with its rhythmical properties that allow it to be read aloud easily, thereby facilitating the 'incorporation' of the text. This rhythmical characteristic is an important reason why *sodoku* cannot merely be equated to 'voiced reading' (as opposed to 'silent reading').

Since the source of all knowledge within the Japanese archipelago came in the form of Chinese writing, the Japanese very early on became accustomed to conducting all forms of scholarship in the Chinese language. *Sodoku*, as a method that required the constant translation and conversion of Chinese text into Japanese, functioned as a crucial tool in acquiring this necessary scholarly skill.

5.3. Chinese as an Intellectual Language

I have described *sodoku* as the 'incorporation' of text and I imagine the process as comparable to that of the language acquisition of a child. Children acquire language by listening to adults and mimicking their sounds. They produce these sounds not only by the movements of the vocal cords, but by the mobilization of the entire body, including the shape of the mouth, the movement of the tongue and jaw, and the breath controlled by the lunges and diaphragm. In other words, language is acquired as a result of the repeated activation of the entire body (Masataka, 2001).

Sodoku resembles the process of language acquisition by children in the sense that it is the process by which one acquires the 'intellectual language' of classical Chinese. The repeated activation of the body in the recitation and mimicking of the Classics would cause these texts to be 'incorporated' to an extent equal to that of one's native language.

Because thinking is an activity of language, I would therefore suggest that the Japanese intellectuals of the early modern period not only wrote and read, but also *thought* in Chinese. The framework of their thinking was constructed on, and restricted by, the patterns of the classical Chinese language and the special vocabulary and concepts of Confucianism. It was only by committing themselves to the Chinese language in this way that they would stand a chance of accessing the truth contained in the sacred scriptures of the Classics.

If we go by Marshall McLuhan's dictum of 'the medium is the message', that is, the idea that the nature of a medium is intrinsically related to the nature of the knowledge it transmits (McLuhan & Carpenter, 1960; Ong, 1982; Tsujimoto, 2010), we may argue that the medium of language dictates the nature of our thinking and the kind of knowledge that can be gained. In that sense, we must also conclude that thought and human development in the early modern period were guided, first and foremost, by the medium of *kundoku*, the 'Japanese reading' of the Chinese language.

6. Confucian Subject Formation

Sodoku was a way of memorizing the Classics by repeated recitation without knowledge of their meaning. While modern pedagogy would surely evaluate it as a coarse method that fails to incite the curiosity and motivation of the students, its merits went unquestioned for centuries.

The early modern period witnessed the establishment of close to 250 domain schools, most of which were constructed after the late eighteenth century, when domains were seeking to implement social and political reforms to deal with the increasingly obvious contradictions inherent in the social order. The fact that these schools—which had been established with the explicit charge of recruiting and fostering human talent to lead social reform—all adopted a curriculum based on Confucian learning, begs the question: Why was knowledge of the Chinese Classics considered useful to contemporary political problems?

The Confucian Classics were regarded as the cumulative knowledge of the Sages, and the words of these Sages were believed to express universal truths. The aim of Confucian education was the 'incorporation' of these truths together with the language and concepts in which they were expressed. Although the 'incorporated' language and knowledge of the Classics might seem to be of no immediate practical use, their function becomes apparent when the subject is faced with concrete problems. When confronted with difficulty, the 'incorporated' texts are intuitively and instantly applied in guiding the behavior of the subject. Confucian knowledge was 'practical' in the sense that it created this kind of strong-willed, and above all, responsible acting subject.[5]

The political activists who played leading roles during the upheavals leading up to the Meiji restoration had all been shaped by this kind of Confucian education. And, as the examples of people such as Sakuma Shōzan 佐久間象山 (1811–1864) and Yokoi Shōnan 横井小楠 (1809–1869)—both of whom advocated the adoption of modern Western science from the basis of their Confucian worldview—show there existed no contradiction between Confucian subjectivity and Western science and technology. Karaki Junzō has remarked that the appearance of self-cultivation idealism (*kyōyō shugi* 教養主義) during Taishō period (1912–1926) signified the 'loss of models' (*kata no sōshitsu*) (Karaki, 1949). From the perspective of this article, I would like to point out that this loss perfectly coincided with the disappearance of the '*sodoku* generation'.

7. Significance to Modern Schooling

Having shown how Confucian ideas of learning are premised upon the mobilization of the body, the characteristics of our modern age become quite clear. Modern schools are based upon 'modern knowledge', that is, objective and transparent knowledge that can be proven through the use of defined concepts and logically structured reasoning. Modern knowledge is not only meticulously divided into different disciplines and fields, the learning curriculum is carefully specified according to age and ability, and evaluations are expressed in clear and discrete percentages. In this system of knowledge, the body is no longer a medium of subject formation, but restricted to the 'scientific body' as taught in biology, the 'active body' as taught in physical education, and the 'healthy body' as taught in health class.

However, we should realize that the body is a part of nature, and moreover, that it is the nature that is closest to us. As such, it is the most direct medium through which we develop ourselves as human beings, and through which we interact with our surroundings—other people, animals, and nature. I would argue that by ignoring the body, modern schooling has, in a sense, inhibited us from engaging with this larger world of perception. The New Education movement, however, rediscovered the usefulness of the body as a tool to learn about emotions, life, and morality and rebelled against modern schooling by placing great emphasis on physical subjects such as music, art, and sports. Although I suspect that the people involved in these educational movements would have denied it, the early modern practice of *sodoku* would fit in well with their outlook on education methods and curricula. A close critical comparison of the commonalities and differences between these two educational views, however, goes beyond the aims of this article.

(Translated by Niels van Steenpaal)[6]

Disclosure statement

No potential conflict of interest was reported by the author.

Notes

1. Since the work is accredited as 'told' (*jutsu* 述) by Mōri Teisai, it is likely that the text was a record of his lectures, noted down by his students, and edited by Teisai himself.
2. There were also schools who took the completion of the *sodoku* track as one of the enrollment criteria. Consequently, students enrolling in these schools would mostly be age 10 and above (Ishikawa, 1976).
3. Ekiken's recommended order in which the Classics should be read is Great Learning, Analects, Mencius, Doctrine of the Mean, Book of History, Book of Odes, Book of Rites, Book of Changes, and the Spring and Autumn Annals, the last two of which Ekiken describes as incredibly hard to read (Kaibara, 1989).
4. Although Ogyū Sorai advocated the ideal of reading the Classics in the original Chinese pronunciation, instead of the 'Japanese reading', he was not opposed to using the 'Japanese reading' in *sodoku* as a method to arrive at the ability of scanned reading (Ogyū, 1994).
5. For this interpretation, I have relied on Miyagi Kimiko's idea of the 'Confucian subject' (Miyagi, 2004).
6. This article is a translation based on a slightly revised version of an article originally published in Japanese (Tsujimoto, 2011).

References

Fuchigami, K. (2009). Kinsei chihō hanju no gakumon keisei to shakai sanka: Tatsuno hanju Matano Gyokusen no gakushū nikki o taishō ni [Academic formation and social involvement of a domainal scholar in the Edo period: An examination of the private study]. *Kyōikushi fōramu Kyōto* [Journal of Matano Gyokusen], *4*, 47–66.

Ishikawa, K. (1976). *Waga kuni ni okeru jidōkan no hattatsu* [The development of conceptions of the child in Japan]. Tōkyō: Seishisha.

Kaibara, E. (1961). Wazoku dōjikun [Precepts for children in colloquial Japanese]. In I. Ken (Ed.), *Yōjōkun, Wazoku dōjikun* (pp. 193–280). Tōkyō: Iwanami shoten.

Kaibara, E. (1989). Dokkei sōran [A guide to reading the Classics]. In T. Inoue (Ed.), *Kaibara Ekiken shiryōshū* (Vol. 1, pp. 15–35). Tōkyō: Perikansha.

Karaki, J. (1949). *Gendaishi e no kokoromi* [An attempt at contemporary history]. Tōkyō: Chikuma shobō.

Masataka, N. (2001). *Kodomo ha kotoba o karada de oboeru* [Children acquire language through their bodies]. Tōkyō: Chūō kōronsha.

McLuhan, M., & Carpenter, E. (Eds.). (1960). *Explorations in Communication: An Anthology*. Boston, MA: Beacon Press.

Miyagi, K. (2004). *Bakumatsuki no shisō to shūzoku* [Thought and customs in Bakumatsu Japan]. Tōkyō: Perikansha.

Ogyū, S. (1994). Yakubun Sentei [A guide for translating]. In Yoshikawa Kōjirō & M. Masao (Eds.), *Ogyū Sorai zenshū* (Vol. 2, pp. 1–433). Tōkyō: Mizusu shobō.

Ong, W. J. (1982). *Orality and literacy*. London: Methuen.

Takeda, K. (1969). *Kinsei nihon gakushū hōhō no kenkyū* [Research on study methods in early modern Japan]. Tōkyō: Kōdansha.

Tsujimoto, M. (2010). Kyōiku no mediashi shiron [An attempt at a media history of education]. In M. Tsujimoto (Ed.), *Chi no dentatsu media no rekishi kenkyū* (pp. 3–25). Kyōto: Shibunkaku shuppan.

Tsujimoto, M. (2011). Sodoku no kyōiku bunka: tekisuto no shintaika [The educational culture of sodoku: The incorporation of text]. In N. Shunsaku, I. Tsuyuhiko, T. Yuichirō, & M. Tsutomu (Eds.), *Zoku 'kundoku' ron: Higashi ajia kanbun sekai no keisei* (pp. 82–105). Tōkyō: Bensei shuppan.

Lixue (理學 *Ihak*) the Lost Art: Confucianism as a form of cultivation of mind

Hyong-Jo Han

Abstract

This article approaches Confucianism as a lost art of living and asks how we can make it relevant again for us. Central to this approach is the cultivation of heart-mind (Xinxue, 心學) designed to help cure ourselves of self-oblivion and self-centeredness so prevalent in our culture today. It is based on the idea of Li (理), the same as Spinoza's God, the absolute Being that has nothing to do with human aspirations at all. To seek this, Li is therefore to gain true freedom. Two preeminent Neo-Confucians of Joseon Korea, Yi Hwang and Yi I, discuss the method of Jing (敬), paying full attention and being watchful, for that end.

1. Introduction

Since the late nineteenth century, our understanding of Korean Confucianism has mirrored its chief nemesis, modernity. The way this unfolded can be divided into three stages:

1. Denial (1890s–1930s): Confucianism was blamed for the loss of Korean sovereignty ('We need to throw it away for the sake of modernization');
2. Excuse (1930s–1980s): *Sirhak* (實學) was fished out of the otherwise 'backward' Confucian tradition and held up as an object of consolation ('Under better circumstances it would've led to modernization'); and
3. Rehabilitation (1980s–1997): Confucianism was identified as the common factor behind the economic rise of the Four Little Dragons and became the code word for 'the East Asian model of modernization' (Among the successful Confucian attributes Western scholars found in this connection were the premium placed on education, the priority of group over individual, and the loyalty to one's superior).

Now, during the past 20 years, this mirror image began to break down. History and tradition were not only an object upon which you would work out your sense of shame or exercise your notion of wealth and power; they have also become a playground just for fun or a resource for all kinds of other personal and social concerns (take ecology for example). We now live in a different society; we have different things to worry about. So we need to look at our Confucian tradition differently. I would like to call this a 'post-Sirhak' perspective.

I am not alone in this. There are other like-minded scholars in Korea who have done valuable work to enlarge this field of vision. It is an on-going work, and the picture is still uncertain. But one thing is clear. They are paying due respect to a variety of other possibilities Confucianism may open up for them. I myself have been interested in how a Confucian way of living could help us overcome some of our modern predicaments, such as alienation.

Cicero said, 'Philosophy is the art of living (*philosophia est ars vitae*)'. In this article, that is what I would like to talk about: Neo-Confucianism as a forgotten art of living. Because of this forgotten aspect, it is sometimes called the Old Learning—*guxue* (古學 *gohak* in Korean). Stressing its training aspect of our heart-mind, it is also called the Heart-mind Learning—*xinxue* (心學 *shimhak*). But the most familiar one is probably the Learning of Principle—*lixue* (理學 *ihak*).

One of the distinguishing characteristics of Joseon Confucianism is its simplified texts and visual aids (diagrams) for the sake of facilitating its practice, which by their nature were widely distributed. The so-called twin peaks of Joseon Confucianism, Yi Hwang (退溪 李滉 1501–1570) and Yi I (栗谷 李珥 1536–1584), produced the representative works in this genre: *The Ten Diagrams on Sage Learning* (聖學十圖) by the former, and *The Secret of Expelling Ignorance* (擊蒙要訣) and *The Essentials of the Studies of the Sages* (聖學輯要) by the latter.

I will be discussing some of these examples in the second half of the article.

2. *Li* (理) as God: Leibniz and Spinoza

Before we get to this 'lost art', I would like to call our attention to how Leibniz understood *li* (理). In his *Discourse on the Natural Theology of the Chinese*, Leibniz said, 'Consequently can we not say that the *li* (理) of the Chinese is the sovereign substance which we revere under the name of God?'[1] I remember how surprised I was when I first read it, because I had always taken *li*'s non-theistic nature for granted, largely under the influence of Dasan Jeong Yak-yong (茶山 丁若鏞 1762–1836). Moreover, it was the Christian missionaries themselves (such as Nicolo Longobardi and Antoine de Saint Marie), who took pains to distinguish Christianity from Chinese thought and denied the latter a 'natural theology'.

Leibniz then defined *li* (理) as 'fundamental reason'. What do we make of this? Here is another quote from his *Discourse*:

> It can be assumed that the Li, Taikie, or Xangti is an intelligent nature which sees all, knows all and can do all. Now the Chinese could not without contradiction attribute such great things to a nature which they believed

to be without any capacities, without life, without consciousness, without intelligence and without wisdom.²

But he went on to stress that these characteristics are not 'anthropopathic, with human forms or dispositions' and that by 'fundamental reason' he does not mean 'an intellectual temperament that can carefully consider what is right'. In other words, *li*(理) imbues *qi* (氣) with form and movement, but the natural process of *qi*(氣) is not based on any decision-making, intended plans, or carefully considered actions of an intelligent agent. Rather, it occurs in 'a form of pre-established harmony', whereby matter continuously moves forward 'due to the natural inclinations of each matter'.

I think this description agrees with Zhu Xi's view of *li*(理). As a matter of fact, Leibniz hit the nail on the head. It was Zhu Xi, who occasionally adopted the traditional language casting *li* and *taiji* (太極, the Supreme Ultimate) in humanized forms. We need to be careful about these expressions of his. The *li* that Zhu Xi talks about lies somewhere between will (有心) and no-will (無心). Referring to *li*, Zhu Xi also used the expression, 'the heart-mind of Heaven and Earth (天地之心)', a will that has nothing to do with anything humanized. At the same time, Zhu Xi would not go as far as to say that there is no will out there, because he didn't want to suggest chaos. So he said: 'If there is no-will (無心), would not a horse give birth to an ox, and plum flowers bloom from peach trees?'³ Zhu Xi therefore made sure to consider will and no-will simultaneously when he discusses *li*. In short, the universe has an order, but the way it formed its character had nothing whatsoever to do with human or humanized will. It is what Leibniz aptly called 'monadic'.

Here Leibniz appears perilously close to negating the very theistic idea of *li* he first conceived as he compared it to the Christian God. For having no 'personality' would rob *li* of the pertaining power and authority under which it intervenes in human affairs; without such personality, it is no more than 'natural order'. This is what Christian theology is deeply concerned about.

This was a matter of no concern to Zhu Xi, however. He was just content to see the workings of *li* behind 'natural order' and 'pre-established harmony'. Even if any 'transcendental' aspect of it is worthy of mention, it has nothing to do with any 'personality' possessing humanized will and telling us what to do or what not to do. Nothing alarmed Zhu Xi more than the idea of *li* as imagined as some kind of personality. He said, 'But now, it should absolutely not be said that a person who makes judgments on transgressions and wickedness is in Heaven'.⁴ You are on your own, so to speak. And Zhu Xi believed you could do it. This is where Neo-Confucianism's strictly internal locus comes from.

Leibniz in the end pulled back and lamented the exclusion of such personality from *li*. While praising Chinese thought for 'newly arous[ing] the natural law engraved in our hearts', he rued that it is 'incomplete' because of its 'lack of Christian revelation and grace which give our original nature a boost toward goodness'. This is disappointing. How could he expect *li* to be endowed with personality when he himself considered its activities to be lacking in human feelings, deliberation and designs?

It was Spinoza, who went all the way. I quote:

> I take a totally different view of God and Nature from that which the later Christians usually entertain, for I hold that God is the imminent, and not the extraneous, cause of all things. I say, All is in God; all lives and moves in God .... The will of God and the laws of nature [are] one.[5]

Does this not sound like Zhu Xi? They both want us to take the world as it is. Right in the eye.

3. *Li*: No Voice, No Face

This *li* then can be distinguished from the Christian God. The path to any 'salvation' it points to is also different from what Buddhism offers. Nor is it in any way close to what Legalists argue, because it denies the primacy of external laws and norms. As Yi Hwang said, 'The Way has no recognizable form, and Heaven is silent'.[6]

Nevertheless, it exists. Where? Here is Yi Hwang again, in a letter to a fellow scholar:

> To proceed in this [Old Learning] you need support from your own close friends, but unfortunately they are too busy doing other things. So sitting all alone in this mountain I often worry if my progress isn't too slow or blocked. As you said, it was a pleasure seeing each other back in those days in Seoul. But I've since come to see how vague and baseless those talks of mine must have sounded at that time. What finally made me see the errors of my ways was Zhu Xi's writing.
>
> This *li* flows right through our daily life. It is present in our ordinary conversations and interactions, and there is not a place where it is absent however little or insignificant things may be. It is what is clearly there before us but without a trace, which makes it so mysterious. Beginners often make the mistake of ignoring this ordinary nature and decide that they should find the truth somewhere high up or far away as if it would deliver them the ultimate prize. Even Zi Gong failed in this. So how could we? Such a search may win the seeker a lot of points of having tried, but I doubt if the quality of his life has actually gotten better. Didn't Li Yanping say, 'The way of this *li* gets ripened entirely in daily living'. The more I chew on his words, the more delicious they taste.[7]

So it is a lot closer than we think. It is present where I wash my face in the morning, where I have my breakfast, where I work (even in a pile of documents on my desk) and so on. That which is here in the fullness of this moment, that which allows this very particularity to be manifest without any external agency, these are some of the things we should be mindful of as we go about our daily living, and that is how we come into contact with *li*. This is what Yi Hwang seems to be saying.

4. *Guxue* (古學 Gohak): Old Learning Sadly Neglected

Pierre Hadot deplored that the philosophy we teach in university is no longer concerned with the art of living, and reminded us of the ancient Greek and Roman spiritual exercises that we lost.[8] I think the same thing can be said about Neo-Confucianism. Here is Yi I:

> Once born as a human being, you must undertake learning (學問). This learning is not something extraordinary or set apart from everyday life; it is actually no more than learning how to deal properly with your daily relations and transactions. It is not about satisfying your vanity or trying to gain some worldly power. If you neglect your learning, weeds will soon spread all over your mind, so to speak, and you will not be able to see things clearly. That is why you must read books and seek *li* (理). Only then would the way be illuminated and your action attain the mean (中).[9]

What Yi I calls 'learning' is a Neo-Confucian code word; it refers to a whole set of program designed to help you 'see things clearly' and 'attain the mean'. It is to be distinguished from two other kinds of learning: worldly learning and anti-worldly learning. The Neo-Confucian learning is neither. As Yi I said, it is to cure us of our age-old amnesia about who we are, and restore our original nature back to us; and this project takes place right in the middle of everyday life.

Surely this is not easy to sell, especially to young people; it has always been, and it will always be. Yi Hwang wrote to the young Yi I:

> There are many talents out there, but it is difficult to find those who are interested in Old Learning. Most just go with the fashion of the moment. Even if we find those who don't, they are either not so talented or too old. But you are in an enviable position of enjoying both talent and youth. So if you start on this path now, who knows how far you will go?[10]

4.1. Decisions (立志)

So, to get initiated into this lifelong project, you need to make up your mind. In other words, you need to make a choice, and that involves renouncing something familiar around you. Like a practicing monk in a remote mountain or in the desert, you need to prepare yourself in such a way that you will now be able to start hearing your inner voice in a new way. Afraid to leave the comforts of the familiar behind, most people are unable to make such a choice.

Yi I said making this choice is none other than your determination to become a sage. And once you did, you need now to reform yourself.

4.2. Reform yourself (革舊習)

What are the things you need to watch out for as you begin? Here is the list Yi I made:

(a) laziness resulting from relying on custom and habit,
(b) inability to sit still,
(c) thirsting after recognition and fame,
(d) ornamental and rote learning,
(e) material obsession and sexual licentiousness.

In short, you need to be able to say No to most of what society holds dear, and make a radical break from them. So, in this sense, the kind of learning Yi I spoke of was exceptional rather than the rule even in Joseon society. Its premise is highly critical to begin with. It warns that most of us are not living well, and that the way we respond to the world is seriously distorted. As Mencius said, no distance is too great for us to have our bent finger straightened, but we pay no such attention to our mind's defect.[11]

4.3. Maintenance (持身)

Under the rubric of 'Small Learning' (小學) Yi I suggests a set of manners and etiquettes to help you. And he provides the following:

(a) keep your speech and thoughts short and simple;
(b) do not let external things (外物) win over you;
(c) and when not attending business or reading, meditate.

5. Xinxue (心學 Shimhak): The Cultivation of Heart-mind

Where do our heart-mind's distortions come from? They come from within us: specifically from self-oblivion and self-centeredness.

5.1. Self-oblivion

Again, Mencius said, 'When their dog or chicken is lost, they go look for it, but when their heart-mind is lost, they don't bother'.[12]

'Who is it that can tell me who I am?' Shakespeare asked through King Lear. And Huineng, one of the ancestral founders of Chinese Chan Buddhism, asked, 'So, what was your original face before your parents were born?' More recently, Lacan questioned the integrity of the 'self' by turning the table on it in his theory of the 'mirror stage' and showing how our ego reflects the desire of the Other.

We commit most of our bad things when we are least conscious. In the *Milinda Panha*, the Buddhist sage Nagasena answers the Indo-Greek king Menander I, 'Sire, the sins we commit in ignorance are greater than the ones we do knowingly'. To the surprised king he gave his explanation: 'Suppose you grab a hot iron ball, first unknowingly and then knowingly. When will you get burned more?'

To this question, the Neo-Confucian response was the word *jing* (敬 *gyeong*). *Jing* is not only an act of paying attention to the matter at hand, but also a state of being fully awake and watchful, so you will be able to restore yourself on a progressive basis. It allows you to be conscious of the present. As the English word, 'conscious', is a compound of 'con' (with) and 'scire' (to know), it refers to being together in the state of knowing. According to Erich Fromm, though, the German word, 'Bewusstsein', conveys this meaning more clearly.[13]

Yi Hwang said that when we continue being attentive, our emotional response (will and desire) and action will start changing so that we get to spend more time with ourselves and become our own master eventually:求放心. I will say more about this *jing* later.

5.2. Self-centeredness (有我之私)

The second source from which our mind's distortions come is self-centeredness. In 1568, two years before he died, Yi Hwang gave the young King Seonjo his last lecture, and the topic he had chosen was 'How to make our rigid self flexible' (訂頑) by Zhang Zai.[14] 'The rigidity of our heart-mind is like a stone', Yi said. Why? It is because of our long-ingrained self-centeredness (有我之私); we are closed off in our blindness.[15] This creates a big problem, because it makes us isolated from the rest of the community we belong to.

The *Analects* tells us how this affliction is formed and reinforced: Confucius cured himself of four afflictions (子絶四), namely,

- (a)　意: partisan will,
- (b)　必: blind lunging ahead,
- (c)　固: repeated tendency or falling into a pattern, and
- (d)　我: ego.[16]

The fact that 'ego' is connected with 'partisan will' indicates a cycle, a vicious one that is (循環不已). What is called ego here refers to what has become 'rigid' in the repeat process of the cycle.

Most of us are not aware that this is where the root of the problem is. It is right in ourselves. This is why Yi Hwang added 'Strike Ignorance (砭愚)' to the title of his last royal lecture. Yi I's *The Secret of Expelling Ignorance* (擊蒙要訣) too was intended for adults, to help them overcome their ignorance (蒙); it was certainly not for children (蒙).

6. Being Attentive, Seeking the Way (居敬窮理)

6.1. 敬, *Paying attention*

As I noted earlier, we are afflicted with two main problems: self-oblivion and hardened, rutted ego. One can go as far as to say that the entire Neo-Confucian program is to deal concretely with these two problems, and the thing that penetrates it right in the center is *jing* (敬 *gyeong*), namely the always mindful, watching, conscious mind.

Originally, this word did not stand alone; it was followed by an object as in 'Worship Heaven (敬天)'. By eliminating the object, the Neo-Confucians gave it a new meaning. The focus now was on yourself.

Jing is, as Yi Hwang said, the linchpin of the whole apparatus 'to break the cycle of ego (私 = 有我之私) and increase the spirit of interconnectedness (公 = 無我之公)'.[17] Until this process gets underway, he would argue, we remain locked in our own cell shouting our own monolog against the wall and judging the world according to our own prejudices; we remain ignorant.

6.2. Investigation of things (格物致知)

Jing will allow us not only to break out of our own prison called ego and connect with others, but also to investigate things and discover them as they are, not according to our own prejudices, not as our own shadows.

It is not an accident that the Neo-Confucians placed this investigation of things at the top of their to-do list. What they sought was objectivity, fully knowing how easily we fall into distorting facts. They had Confucius to quote in this regard, as Will Durant did in the following: '[Men's] thinking is insincere because they let their wishes discolor the facts and determine their conclusions, instead of seeking to extend their knowledge to the utmost by impartially investigating the nature of things'.[18]

7. In Closing

Neo-Confucianism, as expressed in the name, 'Heart-mind Learning' (心學), is about training our heart-mind. This discipline has long been forgotten and now replaced by the so-called 'psychology' imported from the West. The reason why Yi Hwang retired to Tosan was to devote himself to this Old Learning (古學): 'Retired, I am undeservedly at peace, but with my learning sluggish I worry for my old age'.[19]

This Confucian discipline is meant to free our mind of the rigidity inevitably set in from habit and custom, and restore its flexible nature as it originally was. There is no external coercion involved nor any afterlife rewards. What it promises is only the way you are supposed to look like. It is akin to the way a forest sings when the wind blows or the way flowers bloom when spring arrives. As Yi Hwang wrote in one of his songs:

- In a spring breeze, flowers blanket the whole mountain.
- On a fall evening, the moon light chokes the pavilion.
- I don't know what to do with all this fun, day and night.
- Fishes leap, hawks in flight;
- The clouds and sky shine on my pond.

This is no other than the state of human becoming nature (天人合一), a state Yi Hwang aspired to in his old age. This is not mysticism, though it sometimes is criticized as such (especially by those under rationalist persuasion). Yi Hwang would argue that there is nothing mystifying about it (though mysterious its workings may be). On your next visit to Dosan Seowon in Andong, be sure if you haven't gone to see Cheonyeon-dae (天淵臺), a promontory named by him after the line from the *Book of Songs*, '鳶飛戾天, 魚躍于淵'. 'Fishes leap, hawks in flight (魚躍鳶飛)'. To enjoy our daily living in the best possible way sustained by a fountain of vitality—isn't this what the aim of education should be about ultimately?

I close this article with a little episode about Yi Hwang:

Somebody had just passed by Yi Hwang's academy in full view of everyone inside. An old servant burst into a rage, saying 'How rude! He didn't even bother to say greetings nor dismount from his horse!' Yi Hwang replied, 'Why make such a fuss. Didn't the stranger give us a new interesting view?'

Disclosure statement

No potential conflict of interest was reported by the author.

Notes

1. Leibniz (1977, p. 67).
2. Ibid., p. 71.
3. Zhu (1962, v. 1, p. 18).
4. Ibid., 1:22.
5. Durant (1933, pp. 132–133).
6. Yi (1988c, p. 4).
7. Yi (1988d, p. 10).
8. Hadot (1995).
9. Yi (1988f, p. 3).
10. Yi (1988e, p. 39).
11. See *Mencius*. 6: 12.
12. Ibid., 6: 11.
13. Fromm (1994).
14. Yi (1988b).
15. The word 私 here means 'selfish' rather than 'private'. Unlike the usual pair of 'public' and 'private' in Western discourse, whose relationship is often territorial and legalistic, 公 and 私 in Confucian discourse require a different equation.
16. See *The Analects*. 9: 4.
17. Yi (1988b, p. 49).
18. Durant (1954, p. 669).
19. Yi (1988a, p. 47).

References

Durant, W. (1933). *"Spinoza", the story of philosophy*. New York, NY: Simon & Schuster.
Durant, W. (1954). *The story of civilization vol. 1, our oriental heritage*. New York, NY: Simon & Schuster.
Fromm, E. (1994). *The art of being*. London: Bloomsbury Academic.
Hadot, P. (1995). *Philosophy as a way of life*. Oxford: Blackwell.

Leibniz, G. W. (1977). *Discourse on the natural theology of the Chinese*. (H. Rosemont Jr. & J. Daniel Cook, Trans.). Honolulu, HI: University Press of Hawaii.
Yi, H. (1988a). *Collected Works of Yi Hwang, vol. 1*. Seoul: Minjok munhwa chujinhoe.
Yi, H. (1988b). Lectures of evidential learning on the western inscription. In *Collected works of Yi Hwang, vol 7*. Seoul: Minjok munhwa chujinhoe.
Yi, H. (1988c). Preface of 'the ten diagrams on sage learning'. In *Collected Works of Yi Hwang, vol. 7*. Seoul: Minjok munhwa chujinhoe.
Yi, H. (1988d). Reflections on myself. In *Collected Works of Yi Hwang, vol. 14*. Seoul: Minjok munhwa chujinhoe.
Yi, I. (1988e). *The collected works of Yi I, vol. 14*. Seoul: Minjok munhwa chujinhoe.
Yi, I. (1988f). Preface of 'the secret of expelling ignorance'. In *Collected Works of Yi I, vol. 27*. Seoul: Minjok munhwa chujinhoe.
Yi, I., I. (1988). *The collected works of Yi I* (Hanguk munjip chonggan, Vols. 44–45). Seoul: Minjok munhwa chujinhoe.
Zhu, X. (1962). *Classified conversations of master Zhu*, comp. by Li Ching-te. Taiwan: Chung-hua Shu-chu. Photo reprint of 1473 ed.

A Critique of Confucian Learning: On Learners and Knowledge

Ruyu Hung

Abstract

In Confucianism, the subject of learning is one of the most important concerns. For centuries, Confucian thinkers have been devoted to seeking answers to questions such as, how to be a morally noble and decent human being? (成人), how to be a true and moral human being—a noble man? (junzi, 君子) and how to learn to be a junzi? A 'junzi' can be described as 'an ideal person'. For Confucian thinkers, the concept of learning is not only an epistemological problem but also, or perhaps more importantly, an ethical one. Confucian learning can be defined as a particular process of obtaining a certain knowledge in order to become a junzi. The aim of this article is to first introduce the Confucian hierarchy of learning and knowledge. Next, the typology of Confucian knowledge and learners is considered. The author makes a critical enquiry into the Confucian epistemology, and by doing so, attempts to reveal implied limitations and weaknesses. In the final section, the author argues that the Confucian classical text Li Ji revises, in part, the Confucius' hierarchical view of learner and knowledge.

Introduction

For over a 1000 years, Confucianism has greatly influenced how learning takes place, and what is learnt, in the Chinese tradition. Learning (xué) has always been one of the most important issues in Confucianism. As described in the first sentence of the *Analects*, constant learning (xué) brings joy to human lives: 'Is it not pleasant to learn with a constant perseverance and application?' (The *Analects*, Xué Er, 1:1; Legge, 1861).[1] However, who is it, specifically, that enjoys the process of learning? Is everyone capable of appreciating the joyfulness of learning? Furthermore, what is the specific content to be learnt? Definitively, Confucian learning is mainly about self-cultivation (Ivanhoe, 2000; Jiang, 2006; Kim, 2009; Tu, 1978, 1985). The overall doctrine of Confucian learning is targeted at the junzi's self-cultivation. The junzi (君子) refers to the exemplary person in the Confucian doctrine. Translated, the junzi refers to 'a noble person', 'a superior person' or 'a gentleman'. This presents the question, is a person naturally born as a junzi or can they become one? What specific knowledge makes one a junzi? The aim of this article is to explore the issue of learning in relation to the learner and the knowledge from the Confucius viewpoint.

According to Confucius, learners can be classified into four different categories. The criteria for differentiation are the means by which knowledge is gained and the quality of that knowledge. The Confucian ranking raises questions about the nature of learning and knowledge and the relationship between these two concepts, as explained below:

> Those who are born with the possession of knowledge are the highest class of men. Those who learn readily and obtain possession of knowledge, are the next. Those who have difficulties, and yet embrace learning, are the next class. As for those who have difficulties and also do not learn - they are the lowest of the people. (The *Analects*, *Ji Shi* 16:9; modified from Legge's translation, 1861)[2]

According to the above passage, learners are ranked into four levels according to their attitudes towards obtaining knowledge: the highest rated learners are those born gifted, and as such have knowledge without learning. The second-rated group of learners acquire knowledge after learning; the third-rated group experiences difficulties in learning, but manages to overcome them; and those rated at the bottom do not make the effort to overcome the difficulties of learning.

This hierarchy raises such a question as: 'Can the borne knowledge be learned?' As for the third-rated learners, are they not willing to learn or not able to learn? If people can be classified according to the knowledge they possess and the process of obtaining knowledge, can knowledge be classified as well? What is the meaning of the ranking order? When one is seemingly born with knowledge, one is rated in a different class. How then is this class defined? Also, the attitudes towards learning and the result of possessing knowledge are used as criteria by which people are ranked. Yet, what does the concept of knowledge mean? Does the amount of knowledge, or the quality of knowledge, determine its value? The Confucian ranking is a certain regulation affirmed by classification and hierarchy. These questions call our attention to those who are neglected, devalued or excluded from education by the dominant canonical hierarchy. This enquiry aims to outline a deconstructive approach to Confucian learning.

Typology of Learners and Knowledge in Confucianism

As mentioned, the first-rated people could be considered the gifted, those who are born 'knowing'. What then, is this knowledge that these gifted people possess? In my opinion, as in the *Analects*, knowledge can be divided into three categories: ethical or moral knowledge; non-ethical, practical knowledge; and laborious knowledge. Ethical knowledge is that which is of the most value and importance, and is always to be practised in real life. Non-ethical, practical knowledge broadly includes the knowledge of literary studies, administrative talents and articulation. Laborious knowledge refers to the knowledge of hard work involving physical exertion, such as farming, agriculture, forestation, etc.

In Confucianism, the knowledge pertaining to ethics, morality and virtues is always regarded as the most valuable. In one anecdote, Confucius makes a comparison between ethical virtues and practical knowledge:

> A youth, when at home, should be filial, and, outside, respectful to his elders. He should be earnest and trustworthy. He should overflow with love for all, and cultivate friendship with those who are benevolent (ren). When he has time and opportunity, after the performance of these things, he may do literary studies. (*The Analects*, Xue Er 1:6; the author)[3]

In the Confucian doctrine, the learning about ethical virtues is given higher priority than literary studies. Filial piety, respectfulness, earnestness, trustworthiness and benevolence are important virtues in the Confucian morality, whereas literary studies concern the tangible knowledge of literature and writing.

According to Confucius, the highest class of men are born knowing or are in possession of ethical knowledge. They are known as the 'sages' (shèngshién). Confucius says, with modesty, that 'The sage and the man of perfect virtue - how dare I rank myself with them? It may simply be said of me, that I strive to become such without satiety, and teach others without weariness' (*The Analects*, Shu Er 7:34; Legge, 1861).[4] What's more, he says:

> A sage it is not mine to see; could I see a man of real virtue (junzi) that would satisfy me. (The *Analects*, Shu Er 7:26; modified from Legge's translation, 1861)[5]

The sages are rare, born gifted. This gifted knowledge is about morality and ethics. This does not mean that the gifted knowledge is exclusively possessed by the sages. The knowledge that a junzi possesses must also be about ethical knowledge. The junzi can therefore be understood as the people of second ranking—those who possess knowledge through learning. Confucius points out that there are four characteristics of a junzi: '... in his conduct of himself, he was humble; in serving his superior, he was respectful; in nourishing the people, he was kind; in ordering the people, he was just' (The *Analects*, Gong Ye Chang 5:16; Legge, 1861).[6] Humbleness, respectfulness, kindness and justice are ethical virtues. A junzi is the model of an ideal person, with many ethical virtues. These virtues are achieved and nurtured through learning and experience, and it is this learning about ethical knowledge that is given first priority in the Confucian doctrine. Furthermore, the ethical knowledge must be practised in real life. A junzi can only be approved as a junzi once these ethical virtues have been put into practise. The moral traits must not only be spoken in words; they must also be demonstrated in the behaviour of the junzi.

Let me turn to the non-ethical knowledge. Confucius divides his disciples into four categories according to their speciality: virtuous conduct, eloquent speech, administrative talents and literary studies (The *Analects*, Xian Jin, 14:3; Legge, 1861). These specialties can be seen as the parts of non-ethical, practical knowledge.

THE CONFUCIAN CONCEPT OF LEARNING

Yan Yuan (顏淵), one of Confucius' disciples, was distinguished by his virtuous principles and conduct. He is an exemplar of junzi for his enthusiasm of learning and practise of virtues. Once Ji Kanzi asked Confucius who among the disciples had the greatest love for learning. He replied, 'There was Yen Hui (Yan Yuan); he loved to learn. Unfortunately his appointed time was short, and he died. Now there is no one who loves to learn, as he did' (The *Analects*, Xian Jin 11:7; Legge, 1861).[7] Confucius praised Yan Yuan highly for his love of learning and mourned him deeply for his young demise. Regarding attitudes towards learning, Confucius says, 'They who know the truth are not equal to those who love it, and they who love it are not equal to those who delight in it' (The *Analects*, Yong Ye, 6:20; Legge, 1861).[8]

We can derive from the above that there are three different attitudes towards learning: knowing without personal preference or emotion; learning with eagerness and love; and learning with delight. To be able to enjoy learning is deemed the most favourable attitude of a junzi-learner; however, Confucius does not explain under what conditions one would enjoy learning. When he describes a junzi-learner, he often uses Yan Yuan as an example. Yet, the best description of Yan Yuan's love for learning is that he neither directs anger towards others nor does he repeat mistakes. (The *Analects*, Yong Ye, 6:3; Legge, 1861). Confucius does not use the term 'delight' to describe Yan Yuan's state of learning, but Yan Yuan is the best exemplar of a junzi. Therefore, within the category of junzi, it is a prerequisite for a junzi-learner to have a love of learning, but it is even more preferable if the junzi can enjoy the process. Overall, it can be concluded that there are two necessary conditions to cultivate a junzi—the second-rated learner. First, a junzi must possess and practise virtue-related knowledge. Second, a junzi must have a love for learning knowledge relating to virtues.

Next, we will examine non-ethical, practical knowledge. Will it make one a junzi—the second-ranked learner? If one has a love for learning other subjects such as literature, eloquent speech or administration, and, after a period of striving, becomes proficient in one, will they be given the title of a junzi? A careful review of the *Analects* reveals that the Confucian ranking of learners makes very few references to administrative talents. In the passages referring to Ran You (冉有) and Ji Lu (季路 or Zi Lu 子路), Confucius talks about their political administrative abilities. However, Confucius severely castigated Ran You for his policy of raising taxes when Ran You served in the State of Ji. Confucius even said that he no longer saw Ran You as one of his disciples and called on his other disciples to stand against him. Confucius opposed the policy of raising taxes for the unfairness of depriving the people for the sake of the wealthy governor. An administrative talent was hence not considered advantageous for one to be ranked in the second class of junzi.

As for the eloquent-speaking ability, Confucius reiterates more than once that it is insignificant for a junzi to be eloquent or to articulate about knowledge regarding virtues. What makes one indispensably a junzi is that he/she practises the virtues of a junzi. It is the action rather than the words that verifies the truthfulness of the title. As the master says, 'The superior man (junzi) wishes to be slow in his speech and earnest in his conduct' (The *Analects*, Li Ren, 4:24; Legge, 1861).[9] However, even though Confucius shows contempt for eloquence, possession of it could still be advantageous. Confucius uses a term to describe the vice of glib talk: nìng (佞). The word 'nìng' refers to flattery, eloquence and glibness. Confucius would admonish his disciples to keep away from people of nìng. He says: 'Friendship with the man of specious airs; friendship with the insinuatingly soft; and friendship with the glib-tongued - these are injurious.' (The *Analects*, Ji Shi, 16: 4; Legge, 1861)[10] He continues, 'Banish the songs of Zheng, and keep far from erroneous talkers. The songs of Zheng are licentious; specious talkers are dangerous.' (The *Analects*, Wei Ling Gong, 15:11; Legge, 1861)[11] There might be a reason for Confucius' disapproval of glib talk. Once, Confucius talked with Zi Lu, who smartly said that one could directly take the post of a minister without study beforehand. According to Zi Lu, as a minister, one could learn from the experience of making and implementing decisions on policies in relation to common people and land. Thus, the state officer does not need to study to prepare oneself to serve. Without further comments, Confucius simply replied: 'This is why I detest glib talkers' (The *Analects*, Xan Jin, 11:25; Legge, 1861).[12] However, it can be found that in Confucius' view, Zi Lu's seemingly plausible words were a pretext for the lack of preparation of administrators.

Based on the above, among the four categories used by Confucius to classify his students, eloquence in speech and administrative ability would not rank highly as prerequisites for being a junzi. As for ethical virtues and literary studies, if we make a comparison between these two kinds of knowledge, ethical knowledge takes priority over literary studies for a junzi. According to the *Analects*, there are four things that Confucius taught: literary studies, ethical virtues, loyalty and truthfulness (Shu Er, 7:25).[13] Strictly speaking, loyalty and truthfulness should be positioned in the category of ethical virtues. Hence, there are two main subjects that Confucius taught his students: literary studies and virtue-related knowledge. However, Confucius states that though both of them are necessary, they are not sufficient for one to be a junzi. To be a junzi, one must possess the two kinds of knowledge and *practise* them in one's personal actions. Confucius states:

> Where the solid (ethical) qualities are in excess of (formal) accomplishments, we have rusticity; where the accomplishments are in excess of the solid qualities, we have the manners of a clerk. When the accomplishments and solid qualities are equally blended, we then have the man of virtue. (The *Analects*, Yong Ye, 6:18; modified from Legge's translation, 1861)[14]

Confucius uses the term 'zhí' (substance) to denote substantial ethical qualities and the term 'wén' for accomplished formality. The word wén also means 'the literary studies of classics' including rites (禮), music (樂), poetry (詩) and Shu (書). The study of the classics is the means of learning the accomplished formality. Therefore, ethical virtues and literary studies are two crucial areas of learning to become a junzi.

Unlike these two kinds of knowledge, Confucius makes few references to laborious knowledge. Laborious knowledge refers to knowledge that is based on the physical exertion and movement, for example, knowledge of military matters, husbandry and gardening. It seems that only ethical knowledge and literary studies are valuable enough to be discussed thoroughly. Laborious knowledge is too insignificant to be scrutinised by Confucius.

> Fan Chi requested to be taught husbandry. The Master said, 'I am not so good for that as an old husbandman'. He requested also to be taught gardening, and was answered, 'I am not so good for that as an old gardener'. Fan Chi having gone out, the Master said, 'A small man, indeed, is Fan Xu! If a superior man loves propriety, the people will be reverent. If he loves righteousness, the people will submit to his example. If he loves good faith, the people be sincere. Now, when these things are obtained, the people from all quarters will come to him, bearing their children on their backs—what need has he of a knowledge of husbandry?' (The *Analects*, Zi Lu, 13:4; modified from Legge's translation, 1861)[15]

Confucius castigates Fan Chi as 'a small man', for his asking about farming and gardening. In Confucius' mind, with respect to learning, farming and gardening, compared with important virtues like propriety, righteousness and good faith, are of little significance. Confucius' belittlement of laborious knowledge, in my view, can be interpreted in both positive and negative ways. From the positive perspective, we could say that Confucius stresses the value of virtues and sees ethical reflection as more important than the maintenance of livelihood. Confucius' statement echoes with Socrates' maxim that an unexamined life is not worth living. In this regard, laborious knowledge does not have much to do with the examination of life. Yet, from a negative perspective, we can say that knowledge focusing on maintaining livelihood, with practical and realistic purpose, is being unfairly devalued. Confucianism has been widely recognised as a philosophical doctrine, centred on humanity, rather than on objects or the natural world. However, the study of objects and the natural world involves the study of natural sciences and objective attitude, which tends to receive little attention in Chinese intellectual history. Hence, it could be said that the neglect of natural sciences study and pertaining attitudes in the Chinese tradition are intertwined with the Confucian disregard for the study of objects/things.

Concerning learning and knowledge overall, it could therefore be concluded that Confucius differentiates four classes of learners, according to their possession of knowledge and their attitudes towards learning. People of the highest ranking—sages—are the perfect, gifted ones. They are born knowing—and not merely knowing, but in possession of the most important knowledge, that of ethical virtues. Yet, I have doubts regarding the significance of the sage-learner concept for education because, regarding education, this concept proposes that an ideal cannot be attained a posteriori. As for the second-rated learners—the junzi—they are willing to learn and succeed in obtaining knowledge. The knowledge that a junzi possesses includes ethical virtues and literary studies of classics. People of the third class are those who are boxed in by difficult circumstances and strive to escape by learning, while those in the lowest ranking class are in similar circumstances, but devoid even of their own effort to work at finding solutions.

Among these four kinds of learners, the second rated—the junzi—play the most prominent role in the Confucian doctrines. Although Confucius shows great respect for the first-rated people, the sage appears as an unreachable ideal type for ordinary people. The sage is too perfect to approach in real life. Even Confucius himself admits that a sage is too rare to be seen with his own eyes in his limited life. In contrast, the allocation of a junzi is attainable and achievable. Viewed in this way, the Confucian approach to the humanistic learning sets the demanding, yet reachable task of becoming a junzi for learners. As for people of the third and the forth order, Confucius in the *Analects* does not lend much discussion.

Critical Enquiry into Confucian Epistemology

After clarifying the typology or stratification of Confucian learners and knowledge, I intend to make further enquiry into Confucian epistemology and reveal the implied pitfalls.

First of all, we have determined that, according to Confucianism, the ethical virtuous knowledge is deemed the ultimate knowledge. The sage is born knowing and practising virtue. However, I have doubts as to whether one can be born with the knowledge of ethical virtues. In the Confucian view, ren could be seen as the cardinal or comprehensive virtue in relation to other virtues such as trustworthiness (xin), benevolence, loyalty (zhong), filial piety (xiào), righteousness (yì), modesty, honesty, politeness, kindness and so on. The meanings of these virtues lie in human interaction and interpersonal relationships. For example, filial piety (xiào) is one of the most esteemed moral qualities in Confucianism. Filial piety (xiào) refers to one's obedience, support and respect for parents and elders. It can only make sense in the parent–children relationship. Knowledge of this virtue cannot be acquired without first having knowledge of the specific relationship. That the sage is born knowing these virtues infers that he is able to comprehend the meaning of the virtues and to practise them without prior knowledge of interpersonal relationships. An idea such as this seems dubious. If one is arguing for the Confucian position, one might claim that the sage has an inherent inclination towards the virtues. Yet, this is still very ambiguous. There are many different virtues which function when dealing with different interpersonal relationships. There is no reason to claim that all the different kinds of virtues can be brought about because of the same inclination. Moreover, the view of inclination also both oversimplifies and ignores dilemmas or conflicts that are found between different relationships and roles. For example, the ancient sage King Yŭ was described as having devoted himself to work on the dredging channel. According to the legend, he hasn't set foot into his own house for eight years, even if he passed by his home. His devotion, commitment and enthusiasm for the work are not in doubt; however, if Yŭ worked with such extreme dedication, could he have satisfied the roles of father, son or husband as well during this time? The view of the born sage hardly provides a satisfying answer. There is one more critical point of concern: the concept of the born sage suggests that to be one who possesses perfect knowledge, one does not need to make any effort. The gifted one is, by definition, already born to be so. Does this then infer that it is useless and futile to work hard to gain perfect knowledge for any ordinary person? It is impossible for any ordinary person to become a born sage. The concept of the born sage overall does not imply many positive implications for education, which concerns learning a posteriori. It, in fact, presents an unworkable concept for learning.

Secondly, let me shift the focus to the question of knowledge. As we have explored, according to Confucius, the most valuable knowledge is of ethics and virtues. As many scholars point out (Ivanhoe, 2000; Kim, 2009; Tu, 1978, 1985), the Confucian ethic focuses on self-transformation by self-creating and self-directing activities. Yet, its preference for ethical knowledge over other types of knowledge renders the dominancy of humanistic knowledge and the marginalisation of natural sciences and scientific attitudes. As the main focus of the Confucian epistemology is on self-transformation, knowledge of the world, things and non-human beings is treated with little respect. I agree with many scholars (Liu, 2003; Ryan & Louie, 2007) who claim that it is debatable and reductive to make a simple binary between Chinese and Western epistemologies. Compared with modern Western thought, the Confucian epistemology pays less attention to natural sciences and the objective attitude. Relational and interpersonal knowledge is esteemed (Jiang, 2006). Subjective, personal and interpersonal attitudes, implicitly or explicitly, come to the foreground during the process of learning in the Confucian context. Relational knowledge, which tends to be contextualised and is subject dependent or agency dependent, takes priority over objective knowledge, as characterised by the features of objectivity, de-contextualisation, subject independence, repeatability and predictability.

Thirdly, Confucius underestimates the positive effect of experiencing 'difficulties' in learning. As Confucius states, the third-rated learners are those who have difficulties and yet still strive to learn. The lowest-rated learners are those who have difficulties and do not bother to learn. However, in my view, it is too generalised a view because different causes of difficulties in learning have different meaning in an educational context. If the difficulties are due to disability, it is not fair to give reprimand. If the difficulties are caused by an insufficiency of background knowledge or from contemporary psychological viewpoint (Biemans & Simons, 1996; Schallert, 1982; Stevens, 1980), the challenge for a teacher is to help the student acquire the background knowledge, rather than to label one as a third- or lowest-rated learner.

Finally, the Confucian epistemology could be problematic for having scant regard for learners with special needs. As mentioned, some people may be physically or mentally impaired, causing difficulties in learning. They cannot learn nor obtain knowledge, as others do. It seems then that these people are labelled as 'the lowest' simply because of their inherent difficulties. In the *Analects*, Confucius declares, 'teach whoever comes, no matter what or how one is' (The *Analects*, Wei Lin Gong, 15:39; Legge, 1861),[16] but he hardly says anything substantial about education for those who have special needs or disabilities. In fact, special education receives little attention throughout the 2000-year history of Ancient Imperial China (Deng, Poon-Mcbrayer, & Farnsworth, 2001). Although the ancient Confucian text *Li Ji* states 'When the Grand course was pursued ... they showed kindness and compassion to widows, orphans, childless men and those who were disabled by disease, so that they were all sufficiently maintained' (*Li Ji*, Li Yun, 9:1; Legge, 1885),[17] there is hardly any evidence suggesting that substantial and systematic support and education were offered to people with special needs in Ancient China (Deng et al., 2001).

THE CONFUCIAN CONCEPT OF LEARNING

Li Ji's Amendments to the Confucian View of Learning

Based on the above discussion, and within the Confucian tradition, I would like to allocate the second-rated learner with the concept of junzi, and infer that the third-rated learner is meaningful for thinking about education. It has been widely recognised that the junzi is the ideal role model in terms of Confucian educational thought. As for the third-rated learner, he/she is described as one who makes the effort to overcome difficulties faced in learning. In making an effort and endeavouring to obtain knowledge, he/she is a hard-working and diligent learner. However, it seems that Confucius does fully appreciate this diligent learner. A junzi's learning is natural and spontaneous; the junzi does not struggle to learn. For Confucius, the difference between the junzi and the third-rated learner lies in the dynamism of learning activities: for the former, the learning action is initiated effortlessly and spontaneously; and for the latter, the act of learning requires strenuous effort. One may defend the Confucian view that a junzi-learner always has a strong internal motivation to learn. Thus, one does not struggle to set out the learning activity. The third-rated learner's activity is initiated when difficulties are perceived. The point is, the learner is willing to learn, despite the difficulties experienced in doing so. That one is willing to overcome the difficulties is worthy of appreciation. Confucius does not say much about this point; however, another Confucius classic, *Li Ji*, considers learning in a way that is different from what was found in the *Analects*. *Li Ji*, or the *Book of Rites*, is a collection of texts written by Confucius' students and other Confucian scholars in the Warring States period. There are two points of significance in this text. First, it shows approval of the efforts of learners, and second, it states positively that a versatile teacher is capable of teaching all kinds of students.

> The jade uncut will not form a vessel for use; and if men do not learn, they do not know the way (in which they should go). On this account the ancient kings, when establishing states and governing the people, made instruction and schools a primary object; as it is said in the Charge to Yue: 'The thoughts from first to last should be fixed on learning.' (*Li Ji*, Xue Ji, 18:2; Legge, 1885)[18]

Li Ji confirms the importance of learning and points out that learning is motivated by a need to satisfy the deficiency in knowing. Not knowing is itself a difficult circumstance. Hence, learning begins with the perception of difficulties, followed by the attempt to solve them. In this sense, the third-rated learners should not be rated as lower than the junzi. Rather, learners of this kind should be appreciated for their diligence. *Li Ji* resoundingly points out that innocent persons would not know how to go about achieving a good level of learning if they did not have any concept of it (*Li Ji*, Xue Ji, 18:3).[19] Thus, people in a higher position, or in possession of knowledge, have a responsibility to help the innocent to learn. The third section of the *Li Ji*, Xue Ji clearly recognises the positive effect of difficulties in the learning process:

> Therefore when he learns, one knows his own deficiencies; when he teaches, he knows the difficulties of learning. After he knows his deficiencies, one is

able to turn round and examine himself; after he knows the difficulties, he is able to motivate himself to effort. (*Li Ji*, Xue Ji, 18:3; Legge, 1885)[20]

An active learner must be aware of one's own inability to understand the difficulties. Furthermore, this sense of difficulty prompts self-examination, leading to the action of addressing the deficiency. Thus, the process of active learning is grounded in the self-awareness of difficulties and need for self-improvement. *Li Ji* projects a sound and healthy relationship between learning and the difficulties it involves. The following statement supports this viewpoint, by manifesting the engagement of teaching with learning: 'Teaching and learning help each other', as it is said in the *Charge to Yueh*, 'Teaching is the other half of learning'. (*Li Ji*, Xue Ji, 18:3; Legge, 1885)[21] The view of teaching as learning, and that of learning as self-teaching, depicts an organic, mutual, reciprocal and inter-complementary cycle between teachers and students.

Second, if a teacher is truly versatile, he or she is capable of teaching all kinds of students. In this case, it is possible that the third-rated learner, who has difficulties in learning, can be taught to improve. As it is addressed in *Li Ji*:

> When a man of talents and virtue knows the difficulty (on the one hand) and the facility (on the other) in the attainment of learning, and knows (also) the good and the bad qualities (of his pupils), he can vary his methods of teaching. When he can vary his methods of teaching, he can be a master indeed. (*Li Ji*, Xue Ji, 18:11; Legge, 1885)[22]

A good teacher is versatile; he/she has the ability to alternate teaching methods according to the idiosyncrasies of individual students. Some students are smart while some are not. A good teacher will teach in accordance with students' individual differences. Moreover, a good teacher knows well the factors that can hinder or enhance students' learning, and thereby takes the approach of avoiding the hindrance and makes use of the enhancement. A good teacher has to be encouraging but not forceful, guiding but not controlling:

> Thus in his teaching, he leads and does not drag; he strengthens and does not discourage; he opens the way but does not conduct to the end (without the learner's own efforts). Leading and not dragging produces harmony. Strengthening and not discouraging makes attainment easy. Opening the way and not conducting to the end makes (the learner) thoughtful. He who produces such harmony, easy attainment, and thoughtfulness may be pronounced a skilful teacher. (*Li Ji*, *Xue Ji*, 18:9; Legge, 1885)[23]

The above statement shows that the Confucian teacher takes into consideration the difficulties of learning and the individual differences of the learners. The amendment of the *Li Ji* lends the hierarchical view of the learner in Confucianism as more tolerant and resilient. As for the hierarchical view of knowledge, the chapter 'Xue Ji', of *Li Ji*, does not touch upon it. However, it can be concluded that *Li Ji* provides little in the way of a challenge to either the belittlement of laborious knowledge in Confucianism or the esteem of ethical knowledge.

THE CONFUCIAN CONCEPT OF LEARNING

Acknowledgements

I acknowledge the support of the Ministry of Science and Technology (MOST), Taiwan. MOST 104-2410-H-415-016-MY2.

Disclosure statement

No potential conflict of interest was reported by the author.

Notes

1. 學而時習之，不亦說乎？(論語，學而，1:1).
2. 孔子曰：「生而知之者，上也；學而知之者，次也；困而學之，又其次也；困而不學，民斯為下矣。」(論語，季氏，16:9) James Legge translated 困 as dull and stupid. It is not very precise. In my view, one cannot learn well because one is dull and stupid. It is one thing. One cannot learn because one has difficulties. It is another. Legge's translation transmits the meaning that is not implied in the original text.
3. 弟子入則孝，出則弟，謹而信，汎愛眾，而親仁。行有餘力，則以學文。(論語，學而，1:6) I revise the last sentence of Legge's translation. Legge translated 文 into 'polite studies'. Yet 文 can be used to refer to literary studies.
4. 子曰：「若聖與仁，則吾豈敢？抑為之不厭，誨人不倦，則可謂云爾已矣。」(論語，述而，7:34).
5. 子曰：「聖人，吾不得而見之矣；得見君子者，斯可矣。」(論語，述而，7:26).
6. 子謂子產：「有君子之道四焉：其行己也恭，其事上也敬，其養民也惠，其使民也義。」(論語，公冶長，5:16).
7. 孔子對曰：「有顏回者好學，不幸短命死矣！今也則亡。」(論語，先進，11:7).
8. 子曰：「知之者不如好之者，好之者不如樂之者。」(論語，雍也，6:20).
9. 子曰：「君子欲訥於言，而敏於行。」(論語，里仁，4:24).
10. 「友便辟，友善柔，友便佞，損矣。」(論語，季氏，16:4).
11. 「放鄭聲，遠佞人。鄭聲淫，佞人殆。」(論語，衛靈公，15:11).
12. The whole dialogue is as follows: 子路使子羔為費宰。子曰：「賊夫人之子。」子路曰：「有民人焉，有社稷焉。何必讀書，然後為學？」子曰：「是故惡夫佞者。」(論語，先進，11:25).
13. 子以四教：文，行，忠，信。(論語，述而，7:25).
14. 子曰：「質勝文則野，文勝質則史。文質彬彬，然後君子。」(論語，雍也，6:18).
15. 樊遲請學稼，子曰：「吾不如老農。」請學為圃。曰：「吾不如老圃。」樊遲出。子曰：「小人哉，樊須也！上好禮，則民莫敢不敬；上好義，則民莫敢不服；上好信，則民莫敢不用情。夫如是，則四方之民襁負其子而至矣，焉用稼？」(論語，子路，13:4).
16. 有教無類。(論語，衛靈公，15:39).
17. 大道之行也，天下為公。…矜寡孤獨廢疾者，皆有所養。(禮記，禮運，9:1).
18. 玉不琢，不成器；人不學，不知道。是故古之王者建國君民，教學為先。《兌命》曰：「念終始典于學。」其此之謂乎！(禮記，學記，18:2).
19. 雖有至道，弗學，不知其善也。(禮記，學記，18:3).
20. 故學然後知不足，教然後知困。知不足，然後能自反也；知困，然後能自強也。(禮記，學記，18:3).
21. 故曰：教學相長也。《兌命》曰：「學學半。」其此之謂乎！(禮記，學記，18:3).
22. 君子知至學之難易，而知其美惡，然後能博喻；能博喻然後能為師。(禮記，學記，18:11).
23. 故君子之教喻也，道而弗牽，強而弗抑，開而弗達。道而弗牽則和，強而弗抑則易，開而弗達則思；和易以思，可謂善喻矣。(禮記，學記，18:9).

References

Biemans, H. J. A., & Simons, P. R. (1996). Contact-2: A computer-assisted instructional strategy for promoting conceptual change. *Instructional Science, 24,* 157–176.

Deng, M., Poon-Mcbrayer, K. F., & Farnsworth, E. B. (2001). The development of special education in China: A sociocultural review. *Remedial and Special Education, 22,* 288–298.

Ivanhoe, P. J. (2000). *Confucian moral self cultivation.* Indianapolis, IN: Hackett Publishing.

Jiang, X. (2006). The concept of the relational self and its implications for education. *Journal of Chinese Philosophy, 33,* 543–555.

Kim, S. (2009). Self-transformation and civil society: Lockean vs. Confucian. *Dao, 8,* 383–401.

Legge, J. (1861). The Chinese classics. In D. Sturgeon (Ed.), *The Analects* (Vol. 1) 2011. Chinese Text Project. http://ctext.org/analects

Legge, J. (1885). Sacred Books of the East. In D. Sturgeon (Ed.), *The Li Ki* (Vol. 28, part 4) 2011. Chinese Text Project. http://ctext.org/liji

Liu, S.-H. (2003). An integral understanding of knowledge and value: A Confucian perspective. *Journal of Chinese Philosophy, 30,* 387–401.

Ryan, J., & Louie, K. (2007). False dichotomy? 'western' and 'Confucian' concepts of scholarship and learning. *Educational Philosophy and Theory, 39,* 404–417.

Schallert, D. L. (1982). The significance of knowledge: A synthesis of research related to schema theory. In W. Otto & S. White (Eds.), *Reading expository prose* (pp. 13–48). New York, NY: Academic.

Stevens, K. C. (1980). The effect of background knowledge on the reading comprehension of ninth graders. *Journal of Reading Behavior, 12,* 151–154.

Tu, W. (1978). *Humanity and self-cultivation: Essays in Confucian thought.* Boston, MA: Cheng & Tsui.

Tu, W. (1985). *Confucian thought: Selfhood as creative transformation.* Albany, NY: SUNY Press.

Two Concerns of the Confucian Learner

Youn-Ho Park

Abstract

In this article, I trace a shift in Confucian scholars' interpretations about the idea of 'learning for one's self' vs. 'learning for others' from the Analects: a shift from the philological interpretation to the philosophical one. Despite its defect, most Neo-Confucians accepted the philosophical interpretation, because it was considered to play a role of minimizing a newly emerged educational bane, that is, students' exclusively instrumental study for civil service examinations, while establishing the supremacy of 'learning for the cultivation of mind'. I will examine whether this shift would also be said to be valid to contemporary Koreans or East Asians, who are often pictured as exam obsessed.

Confucius and Learning

In the preface to *Historical Record*, Sima Quian (司馬遷, ca. 145 BCE-ca. 86 BCE) commented on the six schools of thought existent at that time. He wrote: 'Confucianism has a wide span of attention, while the gist of it is hard to grasp. So you get little even though after spending many efforts' (Sima, ca. 91 BCE, Preface No. 4). It remains true of the Confucian view of education today. If a contemporary philosopher of education dips into Confucian Classics to figure out its view of education, he would probably be a bit embarrassed, for the Chinese word that can mean the same as the word 'education' appears only once in *the Works of Mencius*.

How about terms like teaching or learning? The ancient Chinese equivalents of teaching, *jiao* (教) appears scattered within Confucian literature, but the numbers are scanty and explanations fragmentary. By contrast, the equivalent of learning, *xue* (學), appears quite often to the extent that you could easily apprehend its central role in Confucian educational thoughts. For instance, the word *jiao* (teaching) appears seven times in *the Confucian Analects*—while the word *xue* (learning) appears 43 times.

It was Confucius who established the central importance of learning in the Confucian mode of life. He was a self-taught man without a fixed teacher, even though he learned from everyone. The driving force of his ceaseless learning was his 'love of learning'—He seldom boasted of himself except when he mentioned of his love of learning (Legge, 1960, 183 & 195). From his teenage to his death, his love of learning was never weakened (*the Analects*, II-4). One might say that the *Analects* itself is full of disciples' memories of Confucius' speeches and deeds as a lover of learning.

Confucius' living model and his footprints influenced many of his disciples and succeeding generations and Confucian scholars' comments and commentaries on learning formed the core of Confucian educational discourses. *Xingli daquan* (性理大全), published in 1415, is a good example. It was a collection of Neo-Confucian articles and comments of more than 120 scholars of Sung (宋) and Yuan (元) China. The part of comments is classified according to the various topics and occupies 45 volumes among total 70 ancient volumes. The topic of learning occupies 14 volumes. 'Teaching others' occupies only one volume. It seems to be considered a part of learning or a form of engagement at the mature stage of learning.

It is significant that the first sentence in the first book of the *Analects* emphasizes the joy of learning: 'Is it not pleasant to learn with a constant perseverance and application? Is it not delightful to have friends coming from distant quarters? Is it not a man of complete virtue, who feels no discomposure though men may take no note of him?' Zhu Xi (朱熹, 1130-1200) annotated the first sentence as follows:

> The meaning of 'learning' is emulation. All human beings are born with good nature, but there is an order of before and after in comprehending it. So the person who comprehends afterward should emulate what the forerunners did. Then he can get enlightened about the good, and can recover his initial state. (Zhu, 1982, 1)

According to Zhu Xi, to learn is to emulate someone. But who is that someone precisely? Zhu Xi answered this question in another place, distinguishing learning in the ordinary sense and learning in the Confucian sense.

> Philologically speaking, the meaning of the letter 'learning' is to emulate the person who knows and performs something well, because the learner himself does not know and does not perform something well. Reasonably speaking, all the activities seeking perfection, being in the state not perfect yet, may be called learning. Even trifling activities like agriculture, archery, horse riding can be an object of learning, because learning can conjoin any activity. However, there is no counterpart of learning here. Then, what is learned on the earth? The person who has just become a scholar is to learn to become a sage. Cheng Yi called this Confucian learning. (Kim, Chi and Yeo, 2009, 19)

In the ordinary sense, learning can happen in all the fields of human activities, and anybody who demonstrates excellence in a field can become a model for others. Therefore, the ordinary meaning of learning is 'to model the master'. But, learning in the Confucian sense limits the range of persons who serve as models. A Confucian model is not a person narrowly developed like a utensil, which has its particular use (*the Analects*, II-12). It should be a person in *omnia paratus* (prepared for all things). Confucius called such a person *junzi* (君子). Confucian scholars aspire to be a *junzi*, a *junzi* aspires to be a sage, a sage aspires to be the heavenly virtues (Liu, 1990, V-60). For instance, Confucius tried to emulate *Zhou*gong (周公) who played a decisive role in laying the cultural foundation of the *Zhou* (周) Dynasty of the ancient China. *Zhou*gong is considered one of the Confucian sages. Mencius, who belongs to the next generation, more boldly asserts the same idea: 'Every human being can achieve the character of Yao (堯) and Shun (舜)' (MENCIUS, 12-2). Thus, Confucian learning is 'to emulate Confucian sages'.

There is one thing to note here. In an additional explanation, Zhu Xi distinguishes two aspects of the sage's character, in terms of both knowledge and deeds. Within this perspective, one's knowledge is considered as a counterpart of one's deeds. Thus, the knowledge that is closely related to or reflects the agent's inwardness was most cherished. This means that 'a split between knowing and doing' was seriously problematized as a symptom of educational failure for Neo-Confucians.

In ancient China, this problem is perceived rather as 'a split between speech and deeds.' In reading the *Analects*, one easily discovers that Confucius himself looks upon embellishing words as a shame and regarded sleight-of-mouth as dangerous (*the Analects*, V-24, XV-10). This was not merely his personal taste; he had good educational reasons for his opposition. The purpose of embellishing words is generally to gain someone's favor. It has nothing to do with self-cultivation. It rather hinders the latter (*the Analects*, I-03). The virtuous should be sure to speak correctly, but those whose speech is good may not always be virtuous (*the Analects*, XIV-05). Therefore, practicing virtuous deeds, not eloquence, has an educational priority. Confucius' advice on speech was that one should try to be a 'man of his word' (*the Analects*, II-13, IV-22, IV-24, XII-03, XIV-29).

Confucius' de-emphasis on eloquence and his subordination of speech to deeds do not indicate that speech was not important in education. Rather, he meant that speech was more useful for social success (*the Analects*, V-04). He once ranked his disciples' strong points as follows:

> Distinguished for their Virtuous principles and practice, there were Yen Yuan (顏淵), Min Tsze-chien (閔子騫), Zan Po-niu (冉伯牛), and Chung-kung (仲弓); for their ability in speech, Tsai Wo (宰我) and Tsze-kung (子貢); for their administrative talent, Zan Yu (冉有) and Chi Lu (季路); for their literary acquirements, Tsze-yu (子游) and Tsze-hsia (子夏) (*the Analects*, XI-02).

'Learning for One's Self' and 'Learning for Others'

In the *Analects*, one of the phrases about learning is meant to contrast the ancient learners with contemporary learners in terms of their concerns and attitudes: 'In ancient times, men learned for themselves. Nowadays, men learn for others' (*The Analects*, XIV-25). Seemingly, Confucius talks about a fact that he recently recognized: learners' concerns and attitudes have changed significantly. From whence had arisen the distinction between 'learning for one's self' and 'learning for others.' But what did he want to say here? It does not seem to be that clear, because his comment was very short without any explanation about the conversational context.

Above all, which side does he take, learning for one's self or learning for others? If we consider his well known 'love of antiquity,' it may be that he takes the side of 'learning for one's self' and criticizes 'learning for others.' But to justify this interpretation, we should make clear what each phrase meant, and consequences resulting from each stance.

There have been two general forms of annotation about the meaning of these two phrases. One is philological, the other is more or less philosophical. He Yan (何晏, n. d.-249) annotated as follows, citing Kong An-guo (孔安國, n. d.-n. d.): Kong An-guo said: 'Minding himself' is to do and practice something in person. 'Minding others' is merely to speak something well.

Another Confucian scholar Xing Bing (邢昺, 932-1010) elucidated it as follows.

> This chapter is talking about the differences between ancient learners and contemporary learners. Ancient men's learning was practiced in person. This is the meaning of 'minding one's self'. Nowadays men's learning emptily explains well for others, but it is not practiced well in person. This is the meaning of 'minding others'. (Xing, 1997, 128)

These two views by the two scholars are almost identical. Learning properly requires both intellectual understanding and active practice. When the active practice is missing or insufficient, it becomes 'learning for others.' The difference lies in whether we go far enough to practice it or limit ourselves to intellectual understanding. 'Learning for others' falls short of 'learning for one self' in that it stops in the middle of the process of learning properly. Each form of learning arrives at a different spot on the same path or direction. What is to be blamed about the form of 'learning for others' is that the priority is mistaken. Learners should concentrate their energy on practicing in person what they know. But the learners for others consume their energy just in showing off their knowledge to others.

Neo-Confucianism emerged on the intellectual stage in the late eleventh century, criticizing both Philological and Literary Confucianism. Neo-Confucians tried to interpret this matter very differently from the earlier interpretations we have just discussed. Let us see Cheng Yi's (程頤, 1033-1107) annotation; 'Minding one's self' is to want 'his own acquisition.' 'Minding others' is to want 'being recognized by others.'

He pays attention to the inner movement of the learner's mind and claimed that ancient learners' minds were focused on their own internal growth, while nowadays learners' minds were focused on gaining others' favors. Each concern goes in the opposite direction, that is, inward or outward; so the former is seen as incompatible with the latter. What consequences would be brought to bear if such different concerns were consistently maintained?

> Cheng Yi said: Ancient learners learned for themselves, but eventually they contributed to the perfection of the world. Nowadays learners learn for others, but they end up losing themselves. (Zhu, 1982, 17)

The consequences are quite radical. Learners for themselves not only become better men, but also contribute to improving the world. On the contrary, learners for others eventually lose themselves, so it will be absurd to talk about their contribution to the world. As a corollary, learning for oneself is preferable, but learning for others is to be condemned, according to Cheng Yi.

However, isn't there some problem with Cheng Yi's interpretation? First of all, there is an inconsistency issue in his annotations.

> Someone asked. Cheng Yi's points in the two paragraphs are not the same. Zhu Xi replied. 'Minding others' in the first paragraph is the lower one, merely wishing to be recognized by others. 'Minding others' in the second paragraph is the higher one, truthfully wishing to help others. However, if you do not start to acquire virtues for your own body and mind, not only can you not help others, but also you lose even yourself in the end. (Kim et al., 2009, 4-473)

One of Zhu Xi's students pointed out that the meaning of 'learning for others' in the second annotation of Cheng Yi's is shifted from its first meaning: 'learning for the recognition of others.' Zhu Xi agreed with this point, and yet defended Cheng Yi's point of view. There are two senses of 'minding others' then. Its first sense can be said to be lower and probably bad, and its second sense, that is, 'learning for helping others' can be said to be higher and well intended. But in spite of one's good intention, 'learning for helping others, not accompanied with learning for himself' is doomed to fail. This means that the act of 'learning for one's self' alone can be really a way of helping others. Even if not intended, one's 'learning for one's self' can exert favorable influences on others involuntarily. A well-known Korean Neo-Confucian scholar, Yi Hwang (李滉, 1501-1570), imagined how it could happen by means of a metaphorical picture of an orchid.

> The learning of *junzi* (君子) is only done for himself. The person who 'minds himself', to quote Zhang Shi (張拭, 1133-1180), is a man who changes the world with his existence itself, but without such an intention. Metaphorically speaking, he resembles an orchid in full bloom which gives off its scent all day long, in a dense forest of deep mount, but not being aware of itself as a source of that scent. The image of this orchid corresponds to the contention that *junzi* ought to mind himself. (Yi, 1971, 5-228)

Now, we came to know that there are two senses of 'minding others.' Even a Neo-Confucian like Zhu Xi affirmed the value of the higher sense, at least that of its good intention. What about the lower sense? Is one's desire for 'others' recognition' totally unnecessary to him as a learner? The answer by another Korean Confucian called Jeong Yakyong (丁若鏞, 1762-1836) was 'No.' He says:

> But '*junzi* dislikes the thought of his name not being mentioned after his death' [*the Analects*, XV-19]. How *junzi* dislikes good names and reputations? Confucius said, 'Do not be afflicted at men's not knowing me' [I-16], 'Seek to be worthy to be known' [IV-14]. If that, how *junzi* dislikes to be recognized by others? When the Duke of Sheh asked Zi Lu about

Confucius, and Zi Lu did not answer him. The Master said, Why did you not say to him,—He is simply a man, who in his eager pursuit of knowledge forgets his food, who in the joy of its attainment forgets his sorrows, and who does not perceive that old age is coming on' [VII-18]? Indeed, even Confucius wanted to be recognized by others. (Jeong, 1985, 5-596)

Now, we came to know again that it was not Confucius' view to reject 'others' recognition' altogether. It may not even be possible in our actual lives. Cheng Yi's annotation on 'minding others' took its lower sense. However, even that may not be untenable in the face of Confucius' other remarks above. The only possibility to make Cheng Yi's interpretation acceptable is to add a proviso: 'without learning for one's self.' In that case, at least in the Confucian *Weltanschauung*, we can safely condemn 'learning for others,' whether it may take its lower or higher sense. Then, we can say that the real significance of the distinction maybe consists in the establishment of the supremacy of 'learning for one's self.' Through the distinction, the Neo-Confucians established the doctrine that 'learning for one's self' is the most valuable purpose of learning.

Lastly, despite the inadequacies of Cheng Yi's interpretation that learning for others is to lose one's self, why did most Neo-Confucians, including Zhu Xi, accept it without any doubt or criticism? It was because Cheng Yi's definition of 'learning for others' worked well as a sort of antidote against the 'educational bane' of the time, the phenomenon that people try to learn for the sake of passing civil service examinations.

The civil service examination system was a basic social institution which selected government officials by testing applicants' knowledge and literal capabilities. As this system took roots, nobody could ignore or dismiss it if he wanted to participate in the state management. Zhu Xi once said that, even if Confucius had been reborn in our time, he would surely have been interested in taking the civil service examination. As every examinee in all ages wants to get good scores from examiners, the examinee easily runs the risk of taking the attitude of 'learning for others recognition'. And this propensity was developed into an 'educational bane' of the time, that is, the culture of learning for passing the exam.

As already mentioned, one can find the subtitle 'the Learning for the Civil Service Examination' among 15 subtitles on learning in *Xingli daquan* (性理大全). It may be reasonable to read it as the indication that the preparation of civil service examination became a huge 'educational problem' then not to be overlooked. Cheng Yi's definition of 'learning for others' as losing one's self was presumably derived from the common practice of learning for the civil service examination. With this definition, Neo-Confucians could downgrade the educational value of 'learning for the civil service examination' on the one hand, and establish the supremacy of 'learning for one's self' on the other hand, which represented the Neo-Confucian sense of learning in the society then.

Conclusive Remarks

Confucius distinguished the differences in one's concerns and attitudes in regard to learning of the time. The scholars before Neo-Confucianism emerged had found the differences between them as follows: learning for one's self is to be accompanied by practicing the learning in person and learning for others is merely to explain something well to others. Learning properly requires both the intellectual understanding of and the active practice of what is learned. Each activity arrives at a different spot on the same path, not in the opposite direction. But Cheng Yi contrasted both activities as if they are taking opposite directions, and the other Neo-Confucians after him accepted his interpretation with little doubt or criticism. But Cheng Yi's interpretation turns out to be an unreasonable one, contradicting even Confucius' words and deeds.

Why did Cheng Yi venture to go so far as to interpret 'the learning for others' as losing one's self? It was because he wanted to relieve the educational bane of the time, so as to establish the supremacy of the 'Neo-Confucian learning.' From early in the history of Confucianism, there were some worries about the possibility of a split between knowledge and deeds or between knowing and practicing. In Confucius' time, it was perceived as the split between speech and deeds. As Confucius hated and repudiated one's eloquence without practicing the words, Neo-Confucians regarded learning for the civil service examination as a huge obstacle to one's true learning. Because every examinee in all ages wants to get good scores on the exam, he easily falls into the temptation to 'learning of others' recognition'. Cheng Yi's new definition of 'learning for others' as losing one's self was in a sense a shrewd realization of the nature of the newly arising educational problem. This new definition of 'learning for others', despite its defect, was expected to reduce the educational bane of learning for the civil service examinations, while establishing the supremacy of 'learning for one's self' as 'learning for one's inner cultivation.' This is why most of Neo-Confucians, including Zhu Xi, had accepted Cheng Yi's definition almost without doubt.

The distinction between learning for one's self and learning for others played a significant role in the history of Korean education. The 'sarim (士林)' faction, a Neo-Confucian group among the ruling class in Choseon Dynasty in the sixteenth-century Korea, deployed a social movement which criticized learning for others which was subjected totally to the civil service examinations. I would call it a 'Let's learn for one's self' movement. It was divided into two stages of learning. In the first stage, reading and practicing *Little Learning* (小學) was a main activity. In the second stage, a theoretically deep understanding of Neo-Confucianism was emphasized in learning. *Seowon* (書院), a dozen of Neo-Confucian academies, emerged for the early second stage, spreading all over the country in the sixteenth century of Choseon Dynasty.

In the concept of 'learning for one's self', one can find a strong affirmation and support for the intrinsic value of learning, which makes educational activity as an enterprise independent of other enterprises such as politics, economics, etc. The concept of 'learning for one's self' produced a Confucian academy called *seowon* as a place for liberal learning and education. However, once *seowon* obtained social esteem, it expanded very rapidly with many side effects. There had already been about 330 provincial schools called *hanggyo* (鄉校) all over the country in sixteenth-century Korea, which had a 900-year-old tradition. In its heyday, the total numbers of *seowon*, which was only 300 years old, amounted to 900. The government demolished all the *seowons* in 1871 due to the various negative effects, with the exception of 47 places. It is the irony of history.

THE CONFUCIAN CONCEPT OF LEARNING

This historical footprint makes Koreans rethink how to deal with human concerns in learning and education as well as the human desires which underlie our educational practices. From the educational perspective, it is not desirable to pursue others' recognition alone in learning without minding one's self. Its danger is often witnessed in our exclusive and instrumental commitment to the preparation for all kinds of examinations. Yet it is just a potential danger, not always leading us into the danger of losing one's self, as some of the Neo-Confucians told us.

Let me take a quick look at Neo-Confucian sayings about the civil service examinations. The problem with the civil service examinations is not that it would obstruct 'our learning for our selves' as a matter of fact, but that it is likely to snatch learner's attention and to take them away from their commitment to 'learning for themselves' (Hu, 1981, 854). Therefore, the examinee should first ensure that his attention would be directed to 'the learning for his self', and that his time and energy would be distributed with a thoughtful sense of priorities. The proportions proposed for the two activities between learning for one's self and learning for others were 3:1, or 7:3, or even half and half (ibid.). There was even a contention that 'learning for one's self' could help the preparation for the civil service examination (ibid.). Likewise, Neo-Confucians did not prohibit their disciples' preparation for the civil service examinations, nor they could do that in reality. They just warned against its potential danger.

It goes without saying that teachers or parents recommend students to pursue 'learning for one's self.' Students stay in the school only temporarily. Someday they are to leave the school to get on in the world in their lives. The desire to be recognized by others is one of the commonest human desires indeed. In fact, as MacIntyre (2007) pointed out, the people who work at the second front of education, such as administrators or politicians, cannot help utilizing external goods for the realization of internal values of education.

> Practices must not be confused with institutions. Chess, physics and medicine are practices; chess clubs, laboratories, universities and hospitals are institutions. Institutions are characteristically and necessarily concerned with what I have called external goods. They are involved in acquiring money and other material goods; they are structured in terms of power and status, and they distribute money, power and status as rewards. Nor could they do otherwise if they sustain not only themselves, but also practices of which they are the bearers. For no practices can survive for any length of time unsustained by institutions. (MacIntyre, 2007, 194)

Teachers who work at the forefront of education ought to guide students well to experience the internal values of education. However, it is not wise to negate or oppress the students' desire to be recognized by others. Rather, it is more realistic to think that we can induce or channel that desire through a reasonable system of incentives and rewards for the advancement of learning and education. We teachers are tempted to think that a real issue around the idea of learning for one's self vs. learning for others is a matter of 'either/or'. But from a broader perspective, it would be rather a matter of 'priority' or that of the 'right balance'.

Disclosure statement

No potential conflict of interest was reported by the author.

References

Hu, G. [胡廣] (1981). *Xingli daquan* [性理大全], 1415; reprint. Seoul: Gyongmunsa.
Jeong, Y. [丁若鏞] (1985). *Yeoyudang Jeonseo* [與猶堂全書], reprint. Vol. 5. Seoul: Yeogang Publisher.
Kim, D., Chi, J., & Yeo, Y. (2009). trans., *Seju Wanyeok Noneo Jipju Daejeon* [細註完譯論語集注大全]. Vols. 1–4. Seoul: Hanul.
Legge, J. (1960). *Chinese classics: With a translation, critical and exegetical notes, prolegomena, and copious indexes* (2 Vols.). Hong Kong: Hong Kong University Press.
Liu, C. [劉清之] (1990). *Little learning* [小學]. Daejeon: Hakminmunhwasa.
MacIntyre, A. (2007). *After virtue* (3rd ed.). Notre Dame: University of Notre Dame Press.
Sima, Q. [司馬遷] (ca. 91 BCE). *Historical record* [史記], At Chinese Text Project. Retrieved from http://ctext.org/shiji/tai-shi-gong-zi-xu
Xing, B. [邢昺] (1997). Lunyu zhushu [論語注疏]. In Y. Ruan (Ed.), *Shisanjing zhushu* (Vol. 8, pp. 1–181), 1815. Taipei: Yiweninshuguan.
Yi, H. [李滉] (1971). *Jeungbo Toegye Jeonseo* [增補退溪全書], Vol. 5. Seoul: Sunggyungwan University Daedongmunhwayeonguwon.
Zhu, X. [朱熹] (1982). *Noneojibju* [論語集注]. Seoul: Sechangseogwan.

Modern Versus Tradition: Are there two different approaches to reading of the Confucian classics?

Chung-yi Cheng

Abstract

How to read the Confucian Classics today? Scholars with philosophical training usually emphasize that the philosophical approach, in comparison with the classicist and historical ones, is the best way to read the Confucian Classics, for it can dig out as much intellectual resources as possible from the classical texts in order to show their modern relevance. Briefly, the philosophical approach runs as follows: (1) first, to discover or identify the philosophical question inhered in the text; (2) then to reconstruct the line of thinking, reasoning, and argumentation revealed in the text, which will lead to the answer of the question; and (3) finally evaluate the effectiveness of the answer by any possible criticism. In spite of the fact that the philosophical approach does help showing the Confucian classics are of great significance to modern people, some scholars seriously caution that this theorization would alienate Confucianism from its very practical concern about self-cultivation. Accordingly, traditional Confucian scholars adopted an existential approach to reading, that is using their personal experience to read, question, understand, and comprehend the meanings of the text, making their comprehension as something they find in themselves and thus will be at ease in it. So there seems to be a dichotomy between the modern philosophical approach and the traditional existential approach to reading of the Confucian Classics. In this paper, I shall argue that the dichotomy has never existed. In fact, traditional Confucian scholars read the Confucian canon in both the philosophical and existential ways. Song Confucian Zhu Xi's 'Method of Reading' is a case in point. I shall then argue that these two approaches should be irreducible and inseparable so as to form a proper way of reading as well as teaching the Confucian Classics today.

THE CONFUCIAN CONCEPT OF LEARNING

I

How to read the Confucian Classics today? This is the question with which people have concerns with Confucianism must have to face. I, as a scholar who is teaching Chinese philosophy in a university's philosophy department, have been thinking of it over and over for years. So, some of my teaching experiences may give clues about the answer. Last year, I offered the course 'Four Books' to my philosophy major students. After reading through chapter one of *the Analects* (*xue er pian* 學而篇) with them, I gave them an assignment with the question of whether or not there is an apparent message in the chapter? Almost all students replied with a positive answer, that is: the chapter is about Confucian conception of learning (*xue* 學). Some of them even provided a detailed explanation that they can find out the definition of learning, different kinds of learning as well as different ways of learning in the text. Instead of praising their having done a good job, I further asked them the question of whether they would regard themselves as clever than Confucius, for they can analyze the text in such a systematic way while Confucius' sayings are just scattered about in fragments in it. Needless to say, no student dared to claim to be clever than Confucius, but nor did they really consider Confucius as a great philosopher or thinker of the past, not to say a sage. I then suggested them to read the text in a totally different way, to question every single sentence of the text according to their living experiences, and as such they would probably find that even the first sentence of *the Analects* does not make much sense to them. It states: 'Is it not a pleasure, having learned something, to try it out at due intervals?' (學而時習之,不亦說乎? Lau, 1979, p. 3; *the Analects* 1:1) But for students today, learning something in lectures so as to write a paper or to get pass in an examination is quite tough and not happy, even if finally getting a good grade would be a pleasure. So, it is not easy for them to truly understand why Confucius is so pleased with learning. Is it because Confucius is a bookish person?

Indeed there are different approaches to reading the Confucian canon today; each refers to its own particular goal. Classicists aim to get at the 'true' meanings of the texts, thus suggest that the reader need to be equipped with the art of philology so as to be able to overcome the great expanse of time lies between the modern reader and the ancient text. Dai Zhen (戴震, 1723–1777), a renowned scholar in philological studies with a great interest in doing philosophy of his day, emphasized the importance of the classicist approach to reading of the Confucian Classics:

> It has been said that there is Han Dynasty classical learning and there is Song Dynasty classical learning: the former emphasizes the ancient glosses (故訓 *guxun*) and the latter is concerned with [understanding] the reason and meaning [of things] (義理 *yili*). I am greatly puzzled by this statement. If one can understand the reason and meaning [of things] by sheer speculation, then anyone can grab them out of emptiness. If that is so, what can we hope to gain from classical learning? It is precisely because sheer speculation cannot lead us to the reason and meaning [of things] as intended by the sages and worthies that one has to seek it from the ancient Classics. When seeking from the ancient Classics, we are facing the huge distance between the ancient and the present that lies in the texts, and then we have

to resort to the ancient glosses [so as to fill the distance up]. Only when the ancient glosses are clear can the Classics be understood, and only when the Classics are understood can the reason and meaning [of things] as intended by the sages and worthies be grasped. (Chin & Freeman, 1990, p. 12, modified; *Dai Zhen Wenji* [戴震文集 *Works of Dai Zhen*] 1980, p. 168)

Here I cannot go into the details of the so-called 'Quarrel between Han and Song learning' (漢宋之爭, *Han Song zhi zheng*) suffice it to say that for Dai, the glosses can provide the true meanings of the Confucian canon. Nowadays, scholars who are working on ancient Chinese literature mainly adopt the classicist approach.

Historians aim to investigate the historical backgrounds from where the Confucian texts arose and how the texts affected history in return. So they may play less attention to the literal meaning of the text; instead they would try to relate the ideas or concepts of the text to the historical circumstances and look into their cause and effect in history. For instance, if we read *the Analects* from the historical point of view, we might contend that the text was obviously served as an ideology for the imperial Han, for the paragraphs 2, 6, 7, 9, and 11 of the first chapter are all about the affirmation of filial piety, which can help cultivating people loyalty to the superior. Among those paragraphs, the second one stands out in relief as strong evidence:

You Zi said, 'Is it rare for a man whose character is such that he is good as a son and obedient as a young man to have the inclination to transgress against his superiors; it is unheard of for one who has no such inclination to be inclined to start a rebellion. The gentleman devotes his efforts to the roots, for once the roots are established, the Way will grow therefrom. Being good as a son and obedient as a young man is, perhaps, the root of a man's character'. (Lau, 1979, p. 3, modified; *the Analects* 1:2)

Also, I cannot engage in detailed explanation of the relationship between filial piety and politicized Confucianism (Liu, 1998, pp. 108–109), which developed as an ideology of Imperial China since two Hans, this will suffice to say that the historical approach to reading of the Confucian texts focuses on their histories rather than their meanings. Nowadays, scholars who are working on ancient Chinese history, in particular the intellectual history, mainly adopt the historical approach.

Philosophers, however, usually like to argue that both the classicist approach and the historical approach fail to achieve the purpose of showing that the Confucian Classics are not something merely archaic but do have their modern relevance. And that only the philosophical approach can help digging out as much intellectual resources as possible from the classical texts and show how they could advise us to cope with our modern problems. For simplicity, I shall borrow the views from Lao Sze-kwong (勞思光, 1927–2012), who published four big volumes of the *History of Chinese Philosophy* (*Xinbian Zhongguo Zhexueshi* 新編中國哲學史), to articulate the philosophical approach as a tripartite one. It runs as follows: (1) first, to discover or identify the philosophical question inhered in the text, that can be one question or a group of questions surrounding a concern or problem. (2) Then to reconstruct the line of thinking, reasoning, and argumentation revealed in the text, which will lead to the answer of the question; and (3) finally evaluate the effectiveness of the answer by any possible criticism (Lao, 1995, pp. 14–17). Using *the Mencius* as an example for illustration:

> My reason for saying that no man is devoid of a heart sensitive to the suffering of other is this. Suppose a man were, all of a sudden, to see a young child on the verge of falling into a well. He would certainly be moved to compassion, not because he wanted to get in the good graces of the parents, nor because he wished to win the praise of his fellow villagers or friends, nor yet because he disliked the cry of the child. From this it can be seen that whoever is devoid of the heart of compassion is not human, whoever is devoid of the heart of shame is not human, whoever is devoid of the heart of courtesy and modesty is not human, whoever is devoid of the heart of right and wrong is not human. The heart of compassion is the germ of benevolence; the heart of shame, of dutifulness; the heart of courtesy and modesty, of observance of the rites; the heart of right and wrong, of wisdom. Man has these four germs just as he has four limbs. For a man possessing these four germs to deny his own potentialities is for him to cripple himself; for him to deny the potentialities of his prince is for him to cripple his prince. If a man is able to develop all these four germs that he possesses, it will be like a fire starting up or a spring coming through. When these are fully developed, he can tend the whole realm within the Four Seas, but if he fails to develop them, he will not be able even to serve his parents. (Lau, 1979, p. 73; *the Mencius* 2A: 6)

Reading this Mencius's famous paragraph from the philosophical point of view, we have first (1) to identify the question Mencius discusses here and that is, the definition of human being. But we should further clarify what sort of definition Mencius looks for? Is it a factual definition or a value definition? (2) Then we shall go into the details of the case that one seeing a child on the verge of falling into a well, asking what exactly the compassionate sentiment (*ce yin* 惻隱) is. Ideally, we can borrow analytic tool from the studies of contemporary moral psychology to examine whether Mencian compassion is reactive distress, like emotional contagion and personal distress, or is concern mechanism like sympathy. Furthermore, is there any empathic or mindreading activity happened in one's mental process of arousing one's compassion?[1] (3) After clearly elucidating the nature of the compassionate sentiment, we shall have to relate it to the other three sentiments, the shame (*xi ue* 羞惡), the courtesy and modesty (*ci rang* 辭讓), and the right and wrong (*shi fei* 是非), asking whether they are four different sentiments of the moral mind, or they are four examples of the manifestation of moral mind, or they are the four aspects that constitute the moral mind, so as to exhibit the moral architecture of the Mencian mind. (4) It may be better to further our study from a comparative horizon to ask the question of whether Mencian philosophy is sentimentalism. (5) And when Mencius maintains that to deny one's own moral potentialities is to cripple oneself (*zizei* 自賊), does he mean that to arouse one's own moral mind is to be aware of oneself? If so, then we shall have to study how the four germs of mind generate self-knowledge (knowledge of one's own mental states) and self-awareness (the ability to identify oneself). In addition, contemporary studies can shed some light on the problem in this regard.[2] Finally, (6) we shall come to the conclusion that Mencius's answer to his question is that human beings are all about having a moral mind and that the moral mind is the essential characteristics of human beings, which differentiates human beings from other animals. But the conclusion is still not the end of the philosophical approach; we have to do the last evaluative job. In other words, we have to question whether Mencius can justify his point by the child case. Is the child case an empirical evidence Mencius uses to prove human beings do universally have a moral mind? If so, how comes a universal conclusion be inferred from a particular premise? Is the child case a moral phenomenon Mencius offers to expose the active human response to others' suffering so as to enable readers to imagine themselves in a similar situation and thus to arouse their moral mind? Let me stop the illustration here. To be sure, I am not going to answer any one of the questions raised above, what I need is just to show what the philosophical approach to reading the text is like.

Although the philosophical approach, in contrast to the classicist and historical approaches, focuses on the thought of the text, it is to be noted that it is the thought of the text but not the reader's own thought. That is to say, the text itself indeed marks the boundary of all possibly appropriate interpretations that could reject over-interpretations as well as 'anything-goes' interpretations. Hence, as philosophical readers we have to respect and not to arbitrarily violate the text lest whatever being read should be nothing to do with the 'true' meaning of the text but for our ideas to be focused on the text. Therefore, the philosophical approach has to take into account three different contexts of reading the Confucian Classics, namely the historical, textual, and reader's ones. To be aware of the historical context is to do something similar to the historical approach, which is to know more about the historical background and development of the text. But we need not be historians and just need to pay enough attention to their concerned studies; and more important, we will definitely look beyond those related histories of the text, for our aim is to do the text philosophically not historically. Unlike intellectual historians, who are interested in the question of who said what, questions of influence, and the historical development of ideas, philosophers are essentially engaged not just with the question of who said what, but with why they say it, did they have good reasons for saying it, what should they have said, and were they right? To be aware of the textual context is to recognize the necessary of the art of philology. Classicists are right to insist that, without the glosses, we cannot understand even a single word in the classical texts, but it does not follow that the glosses can directly provide us with the meaning of the texts. For there is much room for reasoning from words, sentences, paragraphs to the formation of concepts, then to the logical coordination of concepts, and then to meaning. It is this reasoning or philosophical thinking that functions amid literal reading to make interpretation possible. Finally, to be aware of the reader's context is to reflect on our interpretation itself. If we want to let the Confucian Classics telling something meaningful and significant to us, we have to move back and forth in the process of contextualization and decontextualization. We have to contextualize the text in its historical, textual, and logical contexts so as to apprehend its meaning and then to decontextualize it so as to apply the meaning to our present time. In order to yield out the meaning of the text and its application to the fullest, we have to do the process again and again.

In spite of the fact that the philosophical approach can show the classical texts are of great significance to modern people, some scholars seriously caution that this theorizing reading would alienate Confucianism from its very practical concern about self-cultivation. Recently, a significant number of scholars emerged in different areas of Mainland China uphold the return to the Confucian tradition, abandoned the new term 'philosophy', and readopted the old term '*jingxue*' (經學) to characterize their approach to reading the Confucian texts. Accordingly, traditional Confucian scholars adopt a practical (*jianlu* 踐履) and existential (I use it to translate the Chinese term '*xingming*' 性命) approach to reading, using their own personal experiences to read, question, understand, and comprehend the meanings of the texts, which warrants the genuine understanding of meanings by making them their own ones. To this, we might recall what Mencius says as follows:

> Mencius said, 'A gentleman steeps himself in the Way because he wishes to find it in himself. When he finds it in himself, he will be at ease in it; when he is at ease in it, he can draw deeply upon it; when he can draw deeply upon it, he finds its source wherever he turns. That is why a gentleman wishes to find the Way in himself'. (Lau, 1979, p. 177; *the Mencius* 4B: 14)

Hereby reading the Classics is to find in oneself the Way (*zidezhi* 自得之), which is embodied in the meanings of the texts. Therefore, reading especially in an excessive scholastic way must not be an end in itself but merely a means to come to comprehend the Way. It is suggested that one should keep this correct goal in mind so as not to waste one's efforts to strive for something that cannot help exploring one's own way of life. (*xuebujiandao wangfeijingshen* 學不見道, 枉費精神).

Now there seems to be a dichotomy between the philosophical approach and the existential approach; the former is modern, while the latter is traditional. However, I shall argue that this dichotomy has never ever existed.

II

Cheng Yi (程頤, 1033–1107), one of the founders of the Song Ming Neo-Confucianism and the younger brother of Cheng Hao (程顥, 1032–1085), once lamented that ancient sages and worthies had followed rites as normativity (*liyi* 禮義) to nourish their mind but scholars of his day could only resort to meanings (of the Confucian Classics) as normativity (*yili* 義理) to nourish their mind, for they no longer immersed in the ritual circumstances of the past (*Ercheng Ji* [二程集 Works of Two Cheng Brothers] 2004, pp. 162–163). The distinction between *liyi* and *yili* clearly reveals the situation that in Northern Song Confucian scholars already had to promote Confucian thought by reading, studying, and articulating the Confucian texts, given the encounter with Buddhism and Daoism. In fact, Song Ming Confucian scholars recognized that they learned a lot from Buddhism and Daoism, including concepts, ideas, and ways of thinking and practice, while strongly criticized them as not finding the truth (the Way). This is quite similar to our modern situation, for Confucian scholars inevitably have to make a reference to Western philosophy in order to revive Confucianism. As a result of the need to compete with Buddhism and Daoism, Song Ming Confucian scholars unavoidably engaged in detailed exegesis of the Confucian texts, hence it is unimaginable for them not to adopt the philosophical approach or theorizing approach (let's call it TA) to reading. Zhu Xi (朱熹, 1130–1200) even established a rigorous curriculum for the study of the Confucian Classics with a highly elaborated method of reading for his students (Gardner, 1990, pp. 35–56). I have investigated elsewhere Zhu Xi's 'Method of Reading' (*dushufa* 讀書法) from the perspective of philosophical hermeneutics (Cheng, 2010, pp. 28–65), but there is no need to repeat the content here and I shall only quote some sayings from Zhu Xi to show that TA is already a vital ingredient in his method of reading.

In Zhu Xi's 'Method of Reading', we are told:

> In reading, students must first read the classical texts, keeping the commentary in mind, until they can recite the text with complete mastery. As for what appears in the commentary—the explanations of words, the designations and definitions of affairs and things, the elucidations of the Classic's gist, and the passages tying things together—students are to understand it all, as if they themselves had written it; only then will they be able to appreciate the full flavor of the Classic and advance in their learning, experiencing a breakthrough. (Gardner, 1990, p. 156; *Zhuzi Yulei* [朱子語類 *Conversations with Master Zhu*], 1994, p. 191)

It is pretty clear that TA will necessarily involve the kind of historical and philological work. In order to get at the literal meaning of the text, we should resort to glosses and commentaries, for they can offer us the explanations of words, the designations and definitions of affairs and things contained in the text. Zhu Xi himself indeed borrowed many philological views from the two Hans scholarship in his *Commentaries on Four Books* (*Sishu Zhangju Jizhu* 四書章句集注). The literal meaning of the text falls short of understanding, however. So, we must then read the text carefully from terms to lines; to demarcate concepts; and to logically bring concepts together so as to reach understanding. This process has to be repeated ceaselessly; we have to read and reread, to think and rethink, because it is the only way we can enhance our understanding and get familiar to the text. Zhu Xi says:

> Reading is one way of apprehending the principle in things. Now we must carefully consider each and every paragraph, over and over again. If in one day or two days we read just one paragraph, this paragraph will become part of us. After gaining a solid understanding of this paragraph, we should read the next one. If we go on like this from paragraph to paragraph, after a while we will understand moral principles in its entirety. What's required here is that we never stop thinking, occasionally turning over and over in our minds what's already become clear to us; then, enlightenment may occur, without our specially arranging for it. For though the writing and meaning of a text may have been explained in a certain way, each reading

of it will produce its own understanding; thus, with some texts, each reading will lead to a revised understanding. As for those works that have already been definitely explained, with each reading our understanding will become still sounder, and much clearer. Hence I have said: 'In reading, don't value quantity, value only your familiarity with what you've read'. In our efforts to understand what we read, therefore, it's best to advance boldly and not think about retreating. (Gardner, 1990, pp. 133–134, modified; *Zhuzi Yulei*, 1994, p. 167)

In addition, Zhu Xi reminded us the importance of opening or emptying our mind (*xuxin* 虛心), not to be occupied by our old ideas and understanding, so that we can avoid forcing our views on the text and can achieve an objective and appropriate understanding of it. He says:

There is a method for book learning. Simply scrub up and clean the mind, then read. If you don't understand the text, put it down for the moment, wait until your thoughts have cleared, then pick it up and read it again. Now we speak about the need to open up our minds. The mind, how can we open it? We just have to take it and keep it focused on the text. (Gardner, 1990, p. 146, modified; *Zhuzi Yulei*, 1994, p. 177)

He also says that, 'In reading, don't force your ideas on the text. You must get rid of your own ideas and read for the meaning of the ancients.' (Gardner, 1990, p. 150; *Zhuzi Yulei*, 1994, p. 185)

It is equally clear that TA is essentially a virtually dialogic practice. How to ensure that we get an appropriate understanding of the meaning of the ancients? How to know that the meaning of the ancients is right? We have not only to analyze and clarify what the ancients did say about (the Way), but have also to assess and question it. We then, on our own, have to construct what they would say or could say in response to our analysis, assessment, and question. In other words, when reading the classical text we have to hold up both ends of the conversation ourselves and are responsible for taking in it all the directions it needs to go in order to be thorough. Zhu Xi, in this sense, contended that we should be skeptical and doubtful (*yi* 疑) about what you have got in reading: 'In reading, if you have no doubts, encourage them. And if you do have doubts, get rid of them. Only when you've reached this point you made progress' (Gardner, 1990, p. 151; *Zhuzi Yulei*, 1994, p. 186). And while facing with different interpretations, Zhu Xi emphasized that we should unbiasedly examine them and weigh up our options.

The problem students have with reading would be simply that they wish to advance and are unwilling to retreat and reread. The more they advance, the more their reading lacks understanding. It'd be better if they were to retreat but fully comprehend what they read. In general, the problem is that they stick to their opinions and are unwilling to give them up. It's just like hearing litigation: if beforehand the mind supports proposition B, it will simply search for the wrongs in A; and if beforehand it supports A, it will simply discover the wrongs in B. Better to put aside one's views toward A and B and slowly examine both. Hengqu said: 'Wash away the old understanding and bring forth new ideas.' This statement is extremely apt. If one doesn't wash away the old understanding, where will the new ideas arise? (Gardner, 1990, pp. 150–151, modified; *Zhuzi Yulei*, 1994, pp. 185–186)

To conclude, Zhu Xi obviously advocated TA in his method of reading. If one still insists that Zhu Xi is not doing philosophy as the modern reader does, my response would be that it is subject to the usage of 'philosophy.' Here I will not get involve into the trivial debate on whether or not the traditional Chinese thought is a form of philosophy. To me, when Zhu Xi and his students discussed and pondered about how to exactly define even a single term in the Confucian canon, they were doing philosophy, just the same as we do in the modern times.

As we will see, Zhu Xi emphasized the importance of reading the Confucian texts with a practical and existential approach (let's call it EA) as well. In his 'Method of Reading', we read: 'Book learning is a secondary matter of students.' (Gardner, 1990, p. 128; *Zhuzi Yulei*, 1994, p. 161) It is because:

> Book learning is of secondary importance. It would seem that moral principle is originally complete in man; the reason he must engage in book learning is that he hasn't experienced much. The sages experienced a great deal and wrote it down for others to read. Now in book learning we must simply apprehend the many manifestations of moral principle. Once we understand them, we'll find that all of them were complete in us from the very beginning, not added to us from outside. (Gardner, 1990, p. 128; *Zhuzi Yulei*, 1994, p. 161)

For Zhu Xi, the goal of learning is to learn to be a sage, in other words, to learn to be fully human. So, it is not surprised that to him book learning (that meant only to adopt TA to reading) is of secondary importance. The most importance matter, of course, is to make all meanings (of the texts) and reasons (of things revealed in the texts) (*yili* 義理) one grasped from the classical texts turning be something of one's own (that meant to adopt EA to reading). According to Neo-Confucianism, the meaning, reason, principle, or truth (or, in Neo-Confucian terms, *Dao* 道 and *Li* 理) is one, and its manifestations are many (*liyi fenshu* 理一分殊), being in things, matters, humans as well as the sayings of ancient sages and worthies in the Confucian canon. *Dao* (the Way) or *Li* (the moral principle) underlies all things in the cosmos and what it imparts to humans is their good nature or moral mind. Hence, reading the classical texts is nothing but a means toward the end of awakening one's good nature or moral mind so as to comprehend the Way manifested in the whole universe: 'Read books to observe the intentions of the sages and worthies. Follow the intentions of the sages and worthies to observe natural principle.' (Gardner, 1990, p. 129; *Zhuzi Yulei*, 1994, p. 162)

Here we can find that Zhu Xi clearly distinguished EA from TA. To adopt TA to reading is to 'know conceptually' the meanings and reasons embedded in the Confucian Classics, even though they are about the moral principle we should act on and the way of life we should follow. The corollary of this is that TA can offer us merely conceptual knowledge, which does not warrant our change in attitude as well as in our action. By contrast, to adopt EA to reading is to 'embody' the meanings and reasons embedded in the Confucian Classics by using our personal experiences to question the texts. Zhu Xi says:

> When we read the passage 'Is it not a pleasure having learned something, to try it out at due intervals?' we have to ask ourselves: How we have been learning? How we try it out? Have we ever been pleased in learning? We have to experience them. If we only read through the text paragraph by paragraph and getting at the literal meaning, it is useless to us. (*Zhuzi Yulei*, 1994, p. 182)

Indeed this is a dialog with the ancient sages and worthies based on our personal experiences—we have to experience their words personally; only if we made their words our own would they be truly meaningful to us. As mentioned above, TA is essentially a virtual dialog, but that is a conceptual or epistemic dialog. Relative to TA, EA is essentially a virtually spiritual dialog, aiming to make the meanings and reasons embedded in the texts become something we can find in ourselves (*zijia daoli* 自家道理).

> In reading, we cannot seek moral principle solely from the text. We must turn the process around and look for it in ourselves. Since the Qin-Han period, no one has spoken this; people simply have sought it in the text, not in themselves. We have yet to discover for ourselves what the sages previously explained in their texts—only through their words will we find it in ourselves. (Gardner, 1990, p. 149; *Zhuzi Yulei*, 1994, p. 181)

As a result, what EA can offer us is not conceptual knowledge but embodied knowledge, which does warrant our attitudinal changes (beliefs, desires and intentions) and motivate our action.

For Song-Ming Confucianism, the ultimate goal of reading is to learn to be fully human. On this view, there is little doubt that EA is prior to TA, for it can directly lead to the end. More importantly, we may even consider EA as the end in itself, for encouraging one to experience the meaning he has read out of the text is just the same as inviting one to have a moral or spiritual dialog with the text, which will warrant a genuine understanding. And a genuine understanding of the meaning of the text meant understanding it in its actual practice. At times, Zhu Xi even said that after the apprehension of *Dao* or *Li*, one can abandon the classical texts. However, I should add that for Zhu Xi the classical canon is the Wittgenstein's ladder, which is necessary though we may have to abandon it at the end of the day. As to the two approaches to the reading of the classical canon, obviously, in Zhu Xi's method of reading, EA is prior to TA, or EA is of primary importance while TA is of secondary importance, or EA is the end while TA is a means. However, Zhu Xi never mentioned that we can give up TA and merely adopt EA. It is because EA is indeed predicated upon TA; without TA we cannot imagine how EA can go on in its own right. Conversely, without EA, TA will be nothing but a waste of our efforts. (Though

TA may offer us some intellectual pleasure, to Confucianism it is far from the goal of being to be fully human.) It is said:

> Someone asked about not understanding the importance of what's been read. The Master replied: 'How is it that one may understand the importance of what one's reads? Recently, there's been a kind of student who discards the text, hoping to discover the moral principle in one word or half a sentence. There's another kind who reads widely in the texts without understanding their gist. Neither of these types knows how to learn. One must read intimately and reflect intimately, and after a while one will naturally understand moral principle perfectly. If so doing, one will naturally come to understand what you call the "importance of what's been read".' (Gardner, 1990, p. 149; *Zhuzi Yulei*, 1994, p. 182)

All in all, the relationship between TA and EA is: they are irreducible and inseparable (*buji buli* 不即不離). They are irreducible because they are two different approaches; neither the philosophical nor existential approaches can supersede the other. They are inseparable because EA has to be based upon TA and without EA, TA itself cannot serve as an integral part of spiritual exercise and achieve the goal of self-cultivation. To Zhu Xi, self-cultivation itself mainly rests on the efforts to investigate things or affairs and to arrive at knowing (*gewu zhizhi* 格物致知), and the reading of the Confucian Classics is one of the most important ways to do so. Given that Zhu Xi insisted that reading should combine both TA and EA, what one can get from the texts is not merely conceptual knowledge but embodied knowledge that will necessitate the unity of knowing and acting (*zhixing heyi* 知行合一).

Interestingly enough, I find it very similar to what Pierre Hadot reminded us about the ancient Greek conception of philosophy. According to Hadot, the ancient Greek conception of philosophy comprises two parts: philosophy as a philosophical discourse and philosophy as a way of life, and their relationship is:

> They are thus incommensurable –but also inseparable. There is no discourse which deserves to be called philosophical if it is separated from the philosophical life, and there is no philosophical life unless it is directly linked to philosophical discourse. (Hadot, 2002, p. 174)

Here we see how surprisingly the Eastern and Western wisdom converge at the same point. To those who strongly reject the theorization of Confucianism, I would like to quote again Hadot's words as a reminder:

> Conversely, the philosophical life cannot do without philosophical discourse, so long as discourse is inspired and animated by philosophy; for it is an integral part of such a life. We can consider the relationship between philosophical life and philosophical discourse in three different ways, which are closely linked. First, discourse justifies our choice of life and develops all its implications. We could say that through a kind of reciprocal causality, the choice of life determines discourse, and discourse determines our choice of life, as it justifies it theoretically. Second, in order to live philosophically,

we must perform actions on ourselves and on others; and if philosophical discourse is truly the expression of an existential option, then from this perspective it is an indispensable means. Finally, philosophical discourse is one of the very forms of the exercise of the philosophical way of life, as dialogue with others or with oneself. (Hadot, 2002, p. 175)

I believe Zhu Xi would applaud Hadot to the echo.

III

Given the discussion above, I have clearly shown that there is no dichotomy between TA and EA to the reading of the Confucian Classics. However, it does not follow that there is no difference between the traditional and the modern way in respect of reading. The real difference that lies between the traditional and the modern is their different slants to the relationship of TA and EA. For traditional Confucian scholars, even though Zhu Xi and his prominent fellows declared an appropriate understanding, many scholars still tended to overemphasize the inseparability of TA and EA at the expense of the irreducibility. Tang Junyi (唐君毅, 1909–1978), a Confucian philosopher who devoted himself to the reinterpretation of the true spirit of Chinese culture, once in his lecture correctly pointed out that the slant of Confucian scholars of the past poses an obstacle to the building of an objective scholarship for Confucianism, which is the necessary job of the present in order to revive Confucianism (Tang, 1988, pp. 396–397). On the contrary, modern scholars tended to emphasize the irreducibility of TA and EA at the expense of the inseparability. Under the influence of modern Western philosophy, they even argue that the two approaches should be separated from each other. As scholars, they should adopt TA to objectively study Confucian thoughts; whether or not to adopt EA is a personal choice and has nothing to do with their scholarship. So there should be a distinction between the Confucian scholar and the Confucian practitioner. I cannot refute this view here. All I can say here is that if we really want to revive Confucianism, we should recover the ancient wisdom of bringing together both TA and EA to the reading of the Confucian Classics.

Disclosure statement

No potential conflict of interest was reported by the author.

Notes

1. In regard to the studies of moral psychology on human's affective response to other's suffering, see Nichols (2004), pp. 30–64.
2. See Gertler (2011).

References

Cheng, C.-y. (2010). *Ruxue Zhexue Yu Xiandaishijie.* 儒學、哲學與現代世界 [Confucianism, philosophy, and the modern world]. Shijiazhuang: Hebei-Renmin.

Cheng, Y., & Cheng, H. (2004). *Er Cheng Ji* 二程集 [Works of two Cheng brothers]. Beijing: Zhong-Hua.

Chin, A.-p., Freeman, M. (Trans. with a critical introduction). (1990). *Tai Cheng on Mencius: Explorations in words and meaning.* New Haven, CT: Yale University Press.

Dai, Z. (1980). *Dai Zhen Wenji* 戴震文集 [Works of Dai Zhen]. Beijing: Zhong-Hua.

Gardner, D. K. (Trans. with a commentary). (1990). *Learning to be a Sage: Selections from the conversations of master Chu, arranged topically.* Berkeley: University of California Press.

Gertler, B. (2011). *Self-knowledge.* London: Routledge.

Hadot, P. (2002). *What is ancient philosophy* (M. Chase, Trans.). Cambridge, MA: Harvard University Press.

Lao, S.-k. (1995). *Xinbian Zhongguo Zhexueshi* 新編中國史 [History of Chinese philosophy] (Vol. 1). Taipei: San-Min.

Lau, D. C. (Trans.). (1979). *The Analects.* Hong Kong: The Chinese University Press.

Lau, D. C. (Trans.). (1979). *The Mencius.* Hong Kong: The Chinese University Press.

Liu, S.-h. (1998). *Understanding Confucian philosophy: Classical and Sung-Ming.* Westport, CT: Praeger Publishers.

Nichols, S. (2004). *Sentimental rules.* Oxford: Oxford University Press.

Tang, J.-i. (1988). *Zhonghua Renwen Yu Dangjinshijie.* 中華人文與當今世界 [Chinese humanities and the contemporary world]. Taipei: Xue-Sheng.

Zhuzi Yulei 朱子語類 [Conversations with Master Zhu]. (1994). Beijing: Zhong-Hua.

Index

Ames, Roger 17
Analects 6, 13–14, 16, 24–6, 31, 40, 43, 45, 53, 57–61, 81, 85–93, 97–9, 101, 107–8
ancient Greece 23, 27–9, 32–3, 40, 43, 47, 79–80, 116
ancient rhetoric 24, 27–9
Andō Seian 66
Aristotelian ethics 17
art of living 37, 76, 79
autonomy 2, 9, 12, *see also* self-knowledge
awakening 53–4, 57–9, 114

Bildung 4, 23, 37, 39, 43–4, 47–8, *see also* self-cultivation
Blumenbeg, H. 7
book learning, *see* literature studies, reading method
Book of Changes 24
Book of History 24–5
Book of Music 24–5
Book of Poetry, see Book of Songs
Book of Rites 24–6, 31–2, 92–4
Book of Songs 25–6, 29, 82
Boyu 26–32
Bruni, Leonardo 28
Bubules, N. 11
Buddhism 25, 37–9, 45, 66, 78, 80, 111–12

ce yin 109
Chan, Wing-Tsit 38
cheng 60
Cheng, Chung-Yi 5
Cheng, Chung-Ying 4
Cheng Hao 24–5, 111
Cheng Yi 24–5, 98, 100–3, 111
Cheonyeon-dae 82
chess 104
Chi Lu 99
Chinese as intellectual language 70–1
Chin-ssu lu 6, 36–48
Choseon dynasty 103
Christianity 28, 37, 76–8

Chung-kung 99
Chunqiu dynasty 40
ci rang 109, *see also* modesty
Cicero 27–8, 32, 76
citizenship 9
civil service examinations 44–5, 65, 97, 102–4
Classic of Filial Piety 65
classicist approach 106–17
compassion 92, 109
conformism 1–2, 4–5, 8–9, 12–13, 15
Confucian concept of learning: *Chin-ssu lu* 36–48; classical texts 6, 45, 64–73, 89, 97, 106–17, *see also* Four Books, Six Classics, *individual texts*; contrast with Socratic teaching 7–20; critique of 85–94; cultural background 1–3, 8; ethics *see* ethics, moral knowledge; four-dimensional model of learning 52–62; humanistic interpretations 23–33; in Japan 64–73; learning for oneself/others 97–104; modern versus tradition 106–17; teaching for self-knowledge 12–19; typology of learners 86–94
Cox, Harvey 16
Crassus 27
critical thinking 9–12, 16, 19–20

Dai Zhen 107–8
dao 6, 18–19, 57–8, 111–15, *see also* tao
Daoism 25, 111–12
Dasan Jeong Yak-yong 76
Daxue, see Great Learning
De Bary, T. 38–9
de Saint Marie, Antoine 76
Descartes, René 29, 39
Dewey, John 42
disciples of Confucius 8, 14, 17, 26, 31, 87–9, 98–9, 104
Doctrine of the Mean 6, 24–5, 43, 55, 58–61
Durant, Will 82

Earth 39, 77
Edo period 30–1, 64

INDEX

ego 81–2
emoticons 32
Enlightenment 43–4, 47
ethics 7–8, 10–12, 14–15, 17, 24, 28, 38, 56, 86–7, 89–92, *see also* moral knowledge, *zhi*

Fan Chi 90
Fan Xu 90
filial piety 60, 65, 87, 91, 108
Fingarette, Herbert 17–18, 33
Five Classics 43
Foucault, Michel 4, 7, 33
Four Books 24–5, 30, 43–5, 65, 68, 70, 107, 112, *see also individual texts*
Four Little Dragons 75
four-dimensional model of learning 52–62
French Revolution 44
Fromm, Erich 81

Gadamer, H.-G. 24
Germany 29, 37, 43
good conduct 14–15
Gorgias 27
grammar 29–30, 69–70
Great Learning 6, 24–5, 43, 45, 55, 61, 65
Guarino, Battista 30
Guarino da Verona 28, 30
guxue 76, 78–80, 82

Hadot, Pierre 79, 116–17
Hall, David 17
Han, Hyong-Jo 5
Han dynasty 24, 107–8, 112, 115
Hayashi Razan 66
He Yan 100
heart–mind learning 3, 17, 55–6, 58, 75–7, 80–2, *see also xinxue*
Heaven 25–6, 28, 39, 56–9, 77–8, 81
Heidegger, Martin 59
Herbart, J.F. 29
hermeneutics 24
historicism 44
history 27–9
Hon, T.-k. 43
hua 33
Huineng 80
human nature 10–11, 20, 26–7, 43, 59
humanism 2, 5, 23–33, 37, 39, 43, 92
Hume, D. 54
Hung, Ruyu 5
Hwang, Keum-Joong 15

intuitive knowledge, *see liangzhi*
Isocrates 27
Ito Jinsai 24

Japan 3; Confucian education in 64–73; humanism 23–5, 29–31, *see also* Ogyu Sorai

Jaspers, Karl 37
jen 28
Jeong Yakyong 101–2
Ji Kanzi 88
Ji Lu, *see* Zi Lu
jiao 97
jing 80–2
jingxue 111
Joseon Confucianism 76, 80
junzi 3–4, 6, 57–60, 62, 85–91, 93, 98–9, 101

Kaibara Ekiken 65–6, 68
Kaji, N. 31
Kant, Immanuel 59
Karaki Junzō 72
Kato, Morimich 4
kings 33
Kong An-guo 100
Korea 3, 65–6, 103–4
Korean Confucianism 5, 75–82, 101–4
kundoku 70–1
kunten 66
Kwak, Duck-Joo 4

laborious knowledge 86–7, 89
Lacan, Jacques 80
language 2, 4, 24–5, 27–33, 56, 58
language acquisition 71
Lao Sze-kwong 108–9
Latin 27–8, 30
learning for oneself 3, 5, 14, 97, 99–104
learning for others 3, 5, 97, 99–104
lectures 68–70, 81, 107
Leibniz, G.W. 76–8
li 1, 6, 12–20, 31–3, 58, 79, 114–15, *see also* moral knowledge, rites; form of 78–9; as God 76–8
Li, Jin 8
Li Ji, *see Book of Rites*
Li P'an-lung 24
Li Yanping 78
liangzhi 54–6
liberal learning 2–3, 9, 23, 28–9, 31, 103, *see also* humanism
literature studies 26, 28–9, 38, 86–7, 89, 100, *see also* reading method, *wen*
Little Learning 103
Livy 27–8
lixue 76
Longobardi, Nicolo 76
love of learning 40–3
loyalty 60, 75, 89, 91, 108
Lü Zuqian 37

MacIntyre, A. 104
Maintaining Perfect Balance, *see Doctrine of the Mean*
McLuhan, Marshall 71

120

INDEX

meditation 80
memorization 1, 14, 30, 44–5, 67–70
Menander I 80
Mencius 6, 24–5, 43, 45–6, 53–4, 59–61, 80, 97, 99, 109–11
Meno 10
meta-virtues 3, 36, 41, 48
method 29
Min Tsze-chien 99
ming 56
Ming dynasty 56, 66–7, 111–12, 115
modesty 14, 37, 40, 45, 61, 87, 109, 91
moral knowledge 8–12, 15–20, 31, 45–6, 53–5, 86–7, 110, 114–15, *see also* ethics, *li*, *ren*
Mōri Teisai 67
Morohashi, T. 26
music 25–6, 32–3, 73, 89
mysticism 47, 82

Nagasena 80
Nakae Toju 24
Nakamura Tekisai 66–7
Neo-Confucianism 3–4, 36–48, 56, 76–7, 79–82, 99–104, 111, 114
New Education movement 73
ning 88–9
norms 1, 4, 12–13, 16, 18–19, 60, 78

Ogasawara School 31
Ogyu Sorai 23–5, 29–30, 32–3, 69
Old Learning, *see guxue*

parent–child relationship 91, *see also* filial piety
Park, Youn-ho 5
Paul, G. 40
Pestalozzi, J. 29–30
Peters, Michael 8
Petrarch 27–8
Plato 10–11, 27, 37, 40, 43, 46
Pleines, J.-E. 47
poetry 24–9, 32, 56, 70, 89

qi 77
Qin dynasty 115

Ran You 88
reading method 5, 13–16, 30, 38, 112–16, *see also* literature studies
reciting 65, 67–72
reflection 15–20
Reichenbach, Roland 4
ren 3, 6, 12–16, 19, 41, 57, 60–1, 87, 91, *see also* moral knowledge
Renaissance 27–8, 30, 32
rhetoric 24, 27–9
rites 1, 3, 18, 24–6, 31–3, 38, 56, 58, 89, 93–4, 109, 111, *see also li*
ritual propriety, *see li*

Rory, Richard 7
rote learning 1, 14, 44, 80, *see also* memorization
ru 31

sages 7, 13, 38–9, 42, 45–6, 59, 65, 70, 72, 80, 87, 90–1, 99, 107, 111, 114–15, *see also shengxian*
Sakuma Shōzan 72
sarim 103
scanned reading 69
Scholasticism 28–9
second-rated learners 86, 88, 90, 93, *see also junzi*
self-centeredness 81, *see also* ego
self-cultivation 13, 15–17, 37, 40–1, 43, 46–8, 57, 72, 85, 99, 106, 111, 116
self-discipline 1
self-ignorance 9–12, 45, 82
self-knowledge 4, 8–9, 20, 57; Confucian teaching 12–19; Socratic teaching 9–12
self-oblivion 80–1
Seonjo 81
seowon 103
sexuality 33, 80
Shakespeare, William 80
shamanism 31
shengxian 6, 57, 59–60, 87, *see also* sages
Shengzhi 53–4
Shirakawa, S. 31
Shu 89
Sima Quian 97
Sishu daquan 65, 67
Sishu jizhu 65–7
Six Classics 24–5, 68, *see also individual texts*
Small Learning 80
socialization 12, 47
Socratic thought 4, 8–12, 16, 19–20, 37, 39–40, 46, 90; teaching for self-knowledge 9–12
sodoku 65, 67–73
Song dynasty 6, 24–5, 38, 43, 56, 107–8, 111–12, 115
songs, *see* poetry
special education 92
speech 69, 80, 87–9, 99
Spinoza, Baruch 78
Spring and Autumn Annals 24
study manuals 67
subject formation 71–2

taiji 77
Takeda Kanji 68
Tang Junyi 117
tao 7, 13, 17–19, *see also* dao
Taoism 25, 38, 45
text scanning 69
third-rated learners 86, 90–4
tian, *see* Heaven

INDEX

Tokugawa shogunate 24
truthfulness 60, 88–9, 101
Tsai Wo 99
Tsujimoto, Masashi 4, 30
Tsze-hsia 99
Tsze-kung 99
Tsze-yu 99
Tu, Wei-ming 12–13, 15–16
typology of learners 86–94

von Hochheim, Eckhart 39
von Humboldt, Wilhelm 43–4

Wang Shih-chen 24
Wang Yang-ming 38
Warring States period 93
Way, the, *see dao, tao*
wen 6, 58, 89, *see also* literature studies
Western humanism 27–33
Western philosophy 7–8, *see also* Socratic teaching
westernization 2, 4
Williams, B. 10–12
will/no-will 77
Wittgenstein's ladder 115
Works of Mencius, see Mencius

Xing Bing 100
Xingli daquan 98, 102
xinxue 80–1, *see also* heart–mind learning
Xiong Shili 59
xue 6, 52–3, 56–8, 85, 97

Xuezhi 54
Xunzi 53

Yamazaki Ansai 66
Yan Hui 14, 43
Yan Yuan 88, 99
Yen Hui, *see* Yan Yuan
Yi Hwang 76, 78–9, 81–2, 101
Yi I 76, 79–81
Yokoi Shōnan 72
You Zi 108
Yu, J. 8
Yū 91

Zan Po-niu 99
Zan Yu 99
Zhang Shi 101
Zhang Zai 81
zhi 59, 89, *see also* ethics
Zhong Yong, *see Doctrine of the Mean*
Zhou Dunyi 43
Zhou dynasty 99
Zhougong 99
Zhu dynasty 29
Zhu Xi 6, 24–5, 29–30, 32, 37–8, 42–3, 45, 53, 65–7, 77–8, 98–9, 101–3, 112–17
Zhuzi yulei 67
Zi Gong 78
Zi Lu 88–9, 101–2
Zigong 26
Zisi 55
Zixia 31, 58, 62